THE
G.I.F.T.ed
WOMAN

D0786179

SHARON HOFFMAN

LIFE JOURNEY®

Bringing Home the Message for Life

An Imprint of Cook Communications Ministries
COLOARDO SPRINGS, COLORADO   PARIS, ONTARIO
KINGSWAY COMMUNICATIONS, LTD., EASTBOURNE, ENGLAND

Life Journey® is an imprint of
Cook Communications Ministries, Colorado Springs, CO 80918
Cook Communications, Paris, Ontario
Kingsway Communictions, Eastbourne, England

THE G.I.F.T.ED WOMAN
© 2004 by Sharon Hoffman

Published in association with the literary agency of Alive Communications, 7680 Goddard St., Ste. 200, Colorado Springs, CO 80920.

First Printing, 2004
Printed in United States of America
1 2 3 4 5 6 7 8 9 10 Printing/Year 08 07 06 05 04

Cover Design: Kelly Noffsinger

Library of Congress Cataloging-in-Publication Data

Hoffman, Sharon.
  The gifted woman : twelve secrets for a life that impacts eternity / Sharon Hoffman.
      p. cm.
Includes bibliographical references.
  ISBN 0-7814-4065-3 (pbk.)
  1. Women–Religious life. I. Title.
BV4527.H635 2004
248.8'43–dc22

                                        2003027071

To Mrs. Norma Gillming
You have been my steadfast, living object lesson of
a GIFTed woman for over thirty-five years.
Thank you for lifting my chin off my chest,
especially when you gave me permission
"to tribulate in a time of tribulation."
Let us finish our race together with great joy.

And to You, Dear Reader
May this book lead you straight to the heart of our loving,
living God. May you discover the joy that comes from
impacting your world for eternity.

Contents

FOREWORD

I first met Sharon Hoffman when she asked me to speak to the ladies at her church in 1997. I instantly fell in love with this woman and thought to myself, "She is Des Moines, Iowa's best-kept secret!" Now, it's my turn to shine the spotlight on her to America. She is committed to helping women make a dynamic difference in the lives they touch! Let me be the first to tell you I read everything she has written, and you'll be the wiser if you do the same!

Before I go further, let me tell you what I've seen close up when I've been with her. She is warm, loving, sensitive, and eager to express God's love to you as a woman. She is bold and courageous as she opens up her heart and becomes vulnerable where life has been hard. Her early years were not easy. Sharon lost her mother at a very young age and moved around throughout those early formative years. In the classroom of pain the Lord's strength and comfort became real to her (as they do for all of us), an absolute lifeline to Him as the perfect parent. Sharon's new book, *The GIFTed Woman,* simply shares from her heart as an open book the lasting principles the Lord has taught firsthand over her lifetime.

Sharon Hoffman is truly one of the most dynamic Christian women I have ever met. The Lord is using Sharon in a mighty way through her writing and speaking on women's issues. She is vibrant, articulate, and at the same time, tenderhearted towards God.

I always look forward to a new book by Sharon, and this is no exception. Why? Because I always am refreshed and renewed with a sharpened focus to my purpose in serving the living Lord, and am strengthened as a woman who loves Him deeply in the process. *You* will be encouraged if you do the same!

And, as a personal to my friend Sharon Hoffman: "You keep going girl... I'm on your team!"

Barbara Rosberg
Conference Speaker
Co-host of America's Family Coaches—Live! radio program
Author of *Connecting with your Wife*
Co-author of *Divorce Proof Your Marriage, 5 Love Needs of Men and Women, Guard Your Heart, Renewing Your Love,* and *Healing Hurts in Marriage*

INTRODUCTION

Norma Gillming took a huge risk twelve years ago. She invited me to be a workshop leader at the conference her church was hosting.

When I first met Mrs. G, as she is affectionately known by women she has trained all over the world, I would have been the one voted "Least Likely to Ever Speak at the Christian Women's Conference." Thankfully, God has a sense of humor. All along, He had plans for this unqualified, unorganized, oppressed, depressed heart that I could never have imagined. Learning the secrets I write about in this book has changed who I am and how I live my life. It is my prayer that they will do the same for you.

The secrets are not a mantra to memorize or an instant antidote to make all your painful circumstances go away. They are secrets of how God shapes your heart to the image of Jesus Christ so you can influence others to follow God's way as well. This book will reveal twelve key secrets in Scripture that make your life count so you can influence your home, office, marriage, profession—your world! Will you begin as I did by praying, *"God, how can I be a Godly Influencer For Today?"* Simply put, that's the concept of this book. The work that God does in your life can impact so many others. You can be a GIFT—a Godly Influencer For Today. That's exactly what you're about to become as you journey with me through each key word in the secrets. We'll find what really counts for eternity—you and I do.

I hope you will enjoy reading this book as much as I have enjoyed writing it. Take each chapter separately, then see how they fit together as a tapestry. You'll read that I've certainly made my share of mistakes with lots of trial and error. Never once will there be a condemning finger pointing at you. Quite the opposite! I'm right alongside you, praying, cheering you on, honored to be traveling with you on this journey, still learning and growing. While writing, often I've had to slide out of my chair to my knees when confronted by sin. Often I bowed my head to ask for power when God brought a difficult task to mind. I know what it is like to be challenged by the Scriptures and to have to make investments in the lives of others by totally giving myself away. I've learned that the benefits of our becoming Christlike GIFTed women will be felt significantly for generations to come.

Wouldn't you like to wake up every day and live out your life and giftedness in a way that builds up the people around you? If only it were that easy! We can't do this in our own strength. It just can't be done. But God's Spirit indwells us and shapes our experiences so that we grow closer to Him and more like Him. Then we can begin to touch the lives of other people walking the same road.

This book breaks down what might seem like an overwhelming project into manageable, enjoyable disciplines. Here's my hope for you—that as you work your way through the pages of this book you will taste God in such a way that you're sure God's power is enabling you to do the impossible. You will see the once ugly scars of your past as beautiful markings of the Master's hand on your precious life. You will be encouraged to praise and pray as never before. You will join hundreds of women practicing these principles whose hearts are now brave enough to pursue their passion for Jesus Christ. I've seen marriages transformed, entire office atmospheres transformed. Hurting people have changed their addictive behavior and gone out to live lives of purity. Their inspiration came when they purposed to live the GIFTed life.

Over many, many years, Mrs. Gillming, a Bible professor and long-time pastor's wife, has been patiently exhorting, encouraging, and equipping me. Although I was not the most likely candidate to be a women's workshop teacher, she trusted in what God could do with my life. She, in essence, has invested in the lives of thousands now around the globe because she was a GIFT in my life. Individually or along with a study group, you can join many other women who are reading this book and learning more by doing the companion online Bible study for this book at www.sharonhoffman.com. There, you'll get to meet Mrs. G and many other women who will enthusiastically encourage you to practice the principles Christ teaches in His Word.

I bid you let these secrets impact your life; they have changed mine spectacularly! Let God totally transform you. Let His love and grace wrap you up as a GIFTed woman with a beautiful bow on top. You'll never be the same. I will give God all the glory for significantly influencing generations to come.

I'd love to hear from you as you begin investing your life in what really matters—for today and for all eternity.

Warmly,
Sharon

POWER

> A GIFTed woman has access to God's POWER
> to do the impossible.

With God we can do all things; without God we can do nothing.

"Next red light ... I'm outta here. Not just out of this car, but out of everything."

I wanted to taste freedom. Freedom from housecleaning, from laundry, from arguing, from the pain of relationships, and most of all, from the pain of feeling sad. I was starting to look and *feel* really bad. My face looked like a basset hound having a bad day! I was so sad it seemed I wore my "tired hurt" look all the time! I longed for life to be different, to laugh once in a while. My life was taking the breath right out of me. I felt as if I was smothered underneath a pillow stuffed with a lifetime of weighty feathers.

And now, as I was seated in the passenger side of our little Dodge, my hand nervously groped for the door handle. I hung on with all my might, saying nothing to Rob, my husband of seven years, but sighing loud enough for him to know I was upset. Not in seven years had there been so much distance and silence. This two-day getaway was intended to bring us together; instead, hurtful words interfered with a promising romantic weekend.

Where is a red light when you need one? I truly was ready to bolt, even if it meant flinging myself on the pavement and risking my life. It wasn't much of a life like this anyway. What difference would it make? Staying put would mean nothing would change. My eyes blurred with tears, but my mind was clear—or so I thought.

Why couldn't this trip have ended as it began? Our little getaway had actually started out great—in fact we were actually chatting and "connecting." And then, like so many times before, we managed to erupt into a heated quarrel. *Where does that always come from?*

That day in 1979 seems a lifetime ago. Segments of the recollection as I write actually cause me to chuckle instead of cry. A home video of that day would be quite amusing, yet I was hurting. I must confess that I didn't plummet onto the hard concrete that day. I didn't even open the door at the next light and calmly walk into the night. In fact, this became one of those "life moments" when God began to change me.

Looking back, it seemed at the time like my entire life resembled these recurrences. Life would flow smoothly and easily along for a short time, even enjoyable—then, *boom!* I'd become entangled in the dark, difficult threads of hurtful relationships, painful circumstances, or stressful disappointments. And now! Not even my marriage seemed to be turning out like I'd expected. There were days when I thought my heart would break. This particular trip was one of them, and I didn't know what to do. I just wanted out. I wanted to run! Even Rob's attempts at lighthearted conversation seemed to wound and offend me.

God Wasn't Ready to Give Up!

I can't remember everything that happened; I just remember calmness and clarity of thought coming over me. And I remember Rob's voice repeating softly, "Hon, we *are* going to make it. Things *are* going to get better. Things *aren't* as bad as they seem right now. I promise, they will get better."

What did he know that I didn't know? How? And when? And where?

"I don't know all those answers," Rob pleaded, "but I do know that God will help us! He has carried us over rocky patches in the past and he will continue to do so. He didn't bring us this far just to drop us like a box of rocks!" One phrase Rob kept repeating over and over —"With God nothing is impossible"—really seemed to calm me down. Now I'm not one for cheesy little clichés, but at the time, this one really worked! With God nothing is impossible. A little daylight began to break through the clouds of my depressed mind.

At first I didn't want to hear anything that might detour me from my mission of abandonment. I was so determined that my way was the right way. I was hanging on to unbelievably poor advice I had received from well meaning people over the years. A few others had encouraged us to give up, and at times I am astonished that Rob didn't agree.

> Give up on our marriage.
> Give up on our ministry.
> Give up on God.
> Give up on me!

But Rob wasn't ready to give up and neither was God! Rob's continual reassurance turned what I saw as a sure defeat into something of a triumph. Graciously being used of God, he offered again and again, *"We can make it. We are going to make it. Honey, we will make it."*

Rob's "no quit" reassurance slowly began to strengthen my weak faith. I know that God was working in my life because of Rob's reassurance alone. He had every reason to be the one to jump out instead of me. Beyond being irrational and spiritually drained, I was not the wife Rob had bargained for, yet he never gave up on me. His determination for a better marriage began to change my perspective and God's Word began to filter into my worn-out brain.

> There was hope for our marriage.
> Our ministry could and would survive.
> God is almighty and in control.
> And yes, even I could be a better person!

NOTHING IS TOO DIFFICULT FOR GOD

I don't know your background or the situation you find yourself in as you read these lines. I do know this: God is in control. And aren't you glad? On that beautiful autumn day so long ago I was having trouble coming to terms with who was really in charge. As you may have realized, I am not that good at calling the shots. What I realized is that God does a much better job of controlling my life and circumstances than I do. As a young wife I didn't yet understand all that I needed to know about God. But as I grew in my knowledge of Him and trust in Him, I have realized again and again His refuge and strength.

I am grateful that the Lord opened my heart enough to listen to Rob's reassuring words. That night began a path of recovery for me that included restoration and reconciliation. We actually drove straight to our Christian physician's office where I learned to ask for help. His wise counsel gave direction and showed me where to start in reclaiming my sense of wholeness and peace. When I cried out to God, "I can't do this anymore!" He said, "Good, now I can!" The sheer realization of my heavenly Father's love and care for me made me feel special to Him—something I had not felt for a long, long time. Discovering and admitting my weakness was the beginning of finding His abiding strength and healing grace.

That, in essence, is the beauty of the Christian faith. The very thing about to destroy us loses its power over us when we accept the truth that God promises to step in and keep us from jumping! Jude 24 tells us, "Now to Him who is able to keep you from stumbling, and to present you faultless before the presence of His glory with exceeding joy" (NKJV). That could have read, "Now to Him who is able to keep Sharon from jumping ..." You see, God is the source of our power, and we must plug in to Him!

AN ANCIENT STORY OF THE IMPOSSIBLE

The setting is the scrawny Old Testament town of Zarephath. Most of the people have moved on to other places, trying to feed their families. Years without rain had made the ground dry and the air dusty, a truly miserable place to live. The only thing harder to find than food was hope—hope for any future whatsoever.

In Zarephath lived a good and generous mother and son. She found herself in this circumstance without hope. She was planning her last attempt to feed her beloved son with the handful of flour and few drops of oil that were left. Can you imagine such a pitiful sight? Frail and weak from days without food and little water, she would feed her hungry son, then lie down and die. Frightening? Pathetic? Painful? All of these. But remember, with God nothing is hopeless.

God had different plans. And no situation is hopeless when God is at work. The situation and the people involved are not important to this story—it could have been anyone in any town in desperate circumstances. What is important is a weary, faithful woman who dared to risk enough that she stepped out in faith and obeyed in spite what seemed obvious. God sent the prophet Elijah to Zarephath, and he asked this woman for food! Because she obeyed God's instructions, her obedience brought hope. God provided not only the meal for Elijah, but jars of oil and flour that did not run out but continued to feed the woman and her son. Obedience is a key; when you are at the edge of all reason to hope, obedience unlocks the door for blessing and hope to follow. Imagine the woman's sense of well-being and personal value when she realized that God saw and supplied her need. You can read more about this faithful woman in 1 Kings 17:8–16.

How are you responding to struggles, trials, and painful conflicts confronting you right now? Maybe the mortgage is past due, you've lost your job, your kids are sick, your mate has walked out, or the mammogram came back with conspicuous markings! Or maybe right now your biggest hurdle is getting past the piles of laundry, running eleven errands after work, or averting a wreck with a carload of screaming children. It can all be too much! Right now you may be thinking you've got to stop the train and get off quickly. Believe me—I know. Do you handle life's challenges with my old strategy? By jumping?

Jeremiah, a prophet with a bitter message of truth for hearers who did not want to listen, wrote: "I am the LORD, the God of all mankind. Is anything too hard for me? (Jer. 32:27).

God is asking you and me an important question. You may be sitting with me thinking, "Yeah, right! That may be true for some, but my situation is impossible." No! The truth is, God is God and nothing is impossible for Him. God asks, "Is anything too hard for Me?" Our answer should be "absolutely not," but I'm afraid it may be "Well, there's nothing you can't do, God, but I'm really struggling with this, and I don't know how much you can handle!" Think back to our faithful woman in Zarephath. She faithfully obeyed in a hopeless situation, and God supplied. God has not changed in the hundreds of years since her need was met. This day He will do the same for you. The bottom line is, *nothing is too difficult for Him.*

Mentally, fill in the following blank with your own anything(s).

"IS _____ TOO DIFFICULT FOR GOD?"

Whatever you can think of to fill in the blank, no matter how hard it seems, the answer from God will always be "No! There is nothing too difficult for Me!"

WHERE DO YOU BEGIN?

God offers all of us the same promises. He doesn't pick and choose recipients of His blessings. No, on the contrary, we pick and choose which blessings we want to receive. The Bible consistently establishes principles that have worked for generations, and they continue to work today. Yelling, "I want out" has never been one of those principles. Ruth, who lost her husband and worked hard in the hot fields, never called to be let out at the nearest corner. David, as he mustered the courage to face the giant, didn't beg for an open door to escape through. Time and time again God reveals through His Word that in our weakness, He is strong.

Are you tired of putting things off and hoping they will go away? Are you weary from worrying over bills and children and jobs? Have you found, try as you might, that you can't handle everything alone? I never thought I would go through such anguish as to make me want to jump out of a moving car. Physically, I was sick. Emotionally, I was a wreck. The past seven years had been spent in five church positions, raising two young daughters, and moving our personal belongings to nine different homes. My wounds were beginning to get deep. I suspect for some of you the wounds are beginning to get very, very deep. As I speak, I meet women all over our country with the same hurts and pains.

Close your eyes for a moment. Think about what seems the most impossible to you right now. What giant is in your life threatening to slay you? Have you got your slingshot ready? Give it to God. Pour out your deepest disappointments, cares, and anguish. Trust that God will hear you; that He will understand; that He will help. You might be one that benefits from writing your thoughts down in a journal. Put your feelings in black and white. It doesn't have to be fancy or eloquent, only from your heart.

God can handle your thoughts no matter how painfully you express them. In fact, He already knows them and longs to hear you call on Him. This is not powerless psychology. This is merely taking God at His word, which says, "Those who sow in tears will reap with songs of joy" (Ps. 126:5). You will sow many tears as you pour out your heart to God, but He promises the reward will be joy. We learn from Paul in 2 Corinthians 1:3–4 that God is a God of comfort. His strong arm is ready to wrap around your shoulders and His listening ear is reaching to hear your hurts.

Your Added Benefit ... a Godly Influence!

A plus to letting God take control of your life will be the influence you will have on others. In 2 Corinthians 1:4 Paul says that the God of all comfort comforts us "so that we can comfort those in any trouble with the comfort we ourselves have received from God." By taking the focus off of ourselves and putting it onto another person, we take on a quality that is Christlike. Jesus lived so that we may know how to live. He spent thirty-three years influencing the world by spreading the good news that He would bring eternal life. He had already experienced eternal life. But He wanted others to share in it. Jesus influenced others as He traveled, as He walked, even as He slept. We have His example to follow. You have an obligation to influence the world you live in and make a difference in the lives of those nearest to you. Being a wife, a mom, an employee—whatever role you fulfill in life, God has called you for His glory.

Being a **G**odly **I**nfluencer **F**or **T**oday—a GIFTed woman—is not about being perfect. It's about life. It's about living out the life that God has designed uniquely for you, with Him at the controls. Your life will never shine brighter than when you let others know that it's not you, but God, handling your day-to-day problems. Great odds are against all of us. Tremendous forces of darkness and discouragement are trying hard to defeat us. But we will not be moved. God not only will help us to survive, but will help us to make a difference in the world in a great and mighty way.

Remember, jumping never works.

God always does.

SECRET Two

PURPOSE

A GIFTed woman Purposes to live in light of eternity.

Leave the world a better place than you found it!

Happily ever after! That's how all fairy tales are supposed to end, right? Do you remember what you were doing and where you were on the day that Princess Diana was killed in that horrific accident? I sure do. I was filled with shock and grief as I saw the bulletin of her death scroll across the bottom of our TV. As I sat and watched the details of the tragedy unfold, the breath literally squeezed out of my chest. "At four A.M. on the morning of August 31, 1997, after two hours of valiant efforts to save her, Diana, Princess of Wales, was pronounced dead in Paris."

Sixteen scant years earlier 750 million of us had watched this lovely princess's televised fairy tale wedding to Charles,

Prince of Wales. We'll never forget it. The world watched, cheered, toasted, and wept tears of joy for the royal couple. No doubt if you were in my living room during the telecast you would have heard an occasional "ooh and ah" as I was a spectator to the entire splendid event. More than one million eyewitnesses lined the route to the cathedral in England to catch a glimpse of Diana in person.

One of the most incredible sights we all saw was the fairy-like confection of a gown made of bantam-weight crisp ivory silk taffeta and old lace that Diana wore. Hundreds of sequins and seed pearls were sewn by hand. And incredibly, the hand-embroidered 25-foot train seemed to cover most of the carpet in St. Peter's Cathedral. We are told that, for weeks, Diana pinned a long bed sheet to her waist and practiced walking the palace with her awkward train.

Diana's bodice had a wide, frill-edged, scooped neckline and loose, full sleeves tied at the elbows with taffeta bows. The multi-layered tulle crinoline slip propped up the diaphanous skirt. Ivory tulle from her veil glittered with even more hand-sewn sequins. Even her low-heeled pumps were embroidered to match the dress.

Huge bells from St. Peter's reverberated throughout the city for thirty minutes before the princess-to-be and her father arrived in a glistening "glass carriage." After entering the cathedral to the sound of trumpets and pipe organ, the walk down the aisle took three-and-a-half minutes. Prince Charles waited at the end of the long walk with the proud familiar look of a young man welcoming his soon-to-be wife and took Diana's hand. The Archbishop of Canterbury summed up the world's sentiments that day when he stated, "Here is the stuff of which fairy tales are made."[1]

Sixteen wedding cakes, some weighing more than 168 pounds apiece, awaited those who were privileged to attend the wedding reception. A wedding party breakfast, throngs of rose petals, and a kiss on the balcony later—then Prince Charles and his princess bride, Diana, slipped off into the night where the royal train awaited to carry them to three days of honeymooning in the Hampshires.

And they lived happily ever after!

Oh, how the romantic flare in me wishes the story could end with those six words. Diana's own hopes regarding her marriage were recorded when she said, "I had tremendous hope in my heart." If any marriage should have lasted, wasn't it this one? Surely with such a huge investment of creative energy and financial resources the couple could devote the needed effort to make the marriage last. After all, the wedding ceremony itself was insured by Lloyds of London for $22 million. But sadly, no amount of insurance can guarantee a forever-happy ending.

WHAT THE DEVIL FEARS

Whether it's a public figure or a beloved family member, death reminds us all that this life on earth is only temporary. Deciding upon who Jesus is to us personally will determine each one's eternal destiny. That decision drives the very purpose of a GIFTed woman's life. It moves us to want to influence others to know Jesus. It challenges us to achieve our life's aspirations on the basis of what will really last—last forever.

Consider the word *purpose*. Interestingly, the word itself can be either a noun *or* a verb. In this instance I want to use it as a strong action verb because living a life in light of eternity requires exactly what Webster defines *purpose* as: "determine, resolve, commit oneself with a fixed intent, to make up one's mind." Living in an eternal paradigm requires us not just "to think about or half-heartedly aim toward" our lives with a non-temporal focus. Quite the contrary. To live consistently demands that we *purpose* with all our strength and passion to live life focused on an eternal perspective.

That is what a GIFTed woman *purposes* to do with all her heart, soul, and mind. And that's what the enemy fears you are going to do. "Not that I have already arrived and attained that!" the apostle Paul confesses to us (my paraphrasing of Philippians 3:13). Whew! That gives us all encouragement. "But," he goes on to say, "that's what I'm striving for" (again paraphrasing).

With Paul, let's *purpose* to live what's left of our life in a manner worthy of Jesus Christ. Consider how valuable you are to Him—so valuable that He gave up the royal majesty and splendor of His heavenly surroundings to give you the greatest gift of all, His life, for you, on Calvary. The Christ of the cross is the most significant image in history, not only because of His sacrifice for sin, but because of the value He placed on you to be worthy of such a sacrifice. Oh, how He values you. He truly desires a love relationship with you. That's why Paul could be so determined, so committed, and so purposed in his life to live for Christ. I encourage you to make that same choice by an act of your will today, no matter how your past may seem to you. Let's strain ahead, not backward! It doesn't matter who or what you used to be or do. With God's presence inside you, He will do the impossible through you. What you used to think unattainable or unimaginable is possible if you'll purpose to let Him lead you. Why settle for anything less?

Every morning God gives you and me a fresh new day. This is a wonderful gift. His compassions are "new every morning; great is your faithfulness" (Lam. 3:23).

Each day we are blessed with a clean slate. We fill in the blanks as the hours pass. I wonder if we would *purpose* to spend our time today differently if we knew it was to be our last?

What the devil fears most is that you and I will put first things first. He fears that we will make those things that last for Christ and eternity the priority of our lives. He does this in a number of ways. One of Satan's better-known temptations is keeping women "maxed out" in a whirlwind of busyness. After all, a capable woman in the twenty-first century can do it all, can't she? Be wary of living in that deceit! He also loves to attack our motives. *How* and *why* we do things is an indicator of the motivation that drives us. Ask yourself, "What is my motive for doing what I do?" Am I selfishly acting this way to gain others' approval and admiration, so that I can feel good about myself? Our culture presses us into thinking that we have to act to please others. Here it is in a nutshell: If you live for self-pleasure and perfectionism, the enemy has you right where he wants you.

Living for Christ, as Paul explains in Romans 8:28–29, means that the primary *purpose* of all things in our lives is that we may attain Christlikeness. What a wonderful truth to realize that changing diapers, vacuuming, typing, driving a school bus, even reading a book to children can all lead to Christlikeness. What may seem trivial and monotonous to us may be pivotal to our growth in Him. Knowing God has a purpose for my life brings great responsibility with each day that I live regardless of the activities I'm called upon to perform.

Jeremiah 29:11 states, "'For I know the plans I have for you,' declares the Lord, 'plans to prosper you and not to harm you.'" Those words challenge me. I can no longer live according to my dreams, my desires, or my plans. I cannot make decisions based on how I will please people, but how I bring glory to God and fulfill His blessed purpose for my life.

FIRST THINGS FIRST

Take a good look at how you spend your time. Whatever role you fill as a woman—wife, single, mother, career woman, single parent—are the things of eternal consequence at the top?

Getting our priorities right is the first step in living a life of purpose. It helps us make sure that those eternal values take precedence over the urgent activities that seem to make lots of noise in a busy woman's life. Right priorities are so necessary when we are tempted to live in the "survival of the busiest" mode. If we live in that mode, we will spend our lives simply putting out fires of lesser significance that really don't matter. Those fire alarms are always ringing loudly all around us, are they not? But what true GIFTed women are learning about their priorities is that what seemed so urgent last month perhaps doesn't even matter today, when measured in light of eternity.

I remember a time when it seemed my life had no purpose or priorities. I tried, but couldn't even answer my own question: "What is your life's purpose?" I didn't have one. I raced through each day putting out each fire at home, at church, or anywhere I was called. It was exhausting to carry a weighty "I can fix anything" hose around putting out what seemed like four-alarm fires. Before long, I had run dry. Just getting out of bed in the morning began to be a chore because I knew my daily load was going to be overwhelming.

And dinnertime was even more exciting. Rob would open the door and WHAMO! He'd want to go right back out the door. He'd find me discouraged, drowning in disorganization and over-commitments. Instead of greeting him cheerfully, I'd be discouraged, sometimes even in tears. I'm sure it got old day after day hearing, "I'm having a bad day." The truth was, my "I'm having a bad day" really meant, "I'm *making* it a bad day."

Deep within, I long for my purpose to be conforming daily to be more like Jesus inwardly. Outwardly, I long to leave a mark on my family and others that will point them to Jesus Christ. You can discover the invaluable, unique purpose that God designed *just for you. Purpose* in your heart to find and define it. Ask yourself these questions:

What is on my mind when I go to sleep at night and what is the first thing I think of when I wake up?

What breaks your heart and brings you to tears?

What do you daydream about in those rare, quiet moments?

When you read God's Word, are there common themes in the verses you mark?

Have you fulfilled a dream and exclaimed, "Now I know what I was born to do"?

IT'S YOUR EIGHTY-FIFTH BIRTHDAY— WHAT ARE THEY SAYING?

Fast-forward your mind's eye ahead to your eighty-fifth birthday. Picture yourself at your very own eight-fifth birthday party. You've gone through every metamorphosis a woman can face by this age, from matrimony to maternity to maniac! Your entire extended family and many friends have gathered to celebrate. One by one they walk up to a podium in a large hotel ballroom to tell stories and say words about *you,* the guest of honor!

What are they saying? Do they tell anecdotes about you and them having meaningful conversations together? Memories of summer trips taken to the beach, holidays celebrated around home-cooked broccoli casseroles? Do they speak of baton twirling classes and pantyhose loaned in a pinch and Girl Scout cookies in your garage by the caseload and hot chocolate on cold mornings after building a snowman? By the time each loved one takes a turn sharing a chronicle, how are you feeling?

If your family members are as honest and open as mine are, we might all be in trouble! My grown daughters seem to have great recollection when it comes to remembering the trauma that Mother brought upon them during their childhood. Things like, "Mother, I threw up and you weren't home!" or "I needed my cheerleading shoes and you wouldn't get in the car and bring them!" Or perhaps another tender moment like, "I woke up at the church on the back pew where you'd left me asleep. And nobody was there. And the church was locked!" (Before you send Social Services after me, think back a few years; didn't you do any of these same things? Please nod your head.)

Before you have to hear all about it at my eight-fifth birthday party, I must confess here and now to:

- Buying chicken parts instead of saving money and cutting up a whole chicken.

- Ironing only the front and collar of Rob's shirts.

- Not turning my bed mattresses once a year.

- Yes, it is true. Most days you can write your name in the dust on my coffee tables.

- I have been known to cheat at board games to let one of the children win.

What a birthday party I'll have! The stories told at the microphone will sound a lot like a huge guilt trip rather than a celebration. Seriously, reality is that even if there is no party or public testimonials, still you and I are living a life before others that shouts loud and clear what we count dear in this life. All kidding aside, will your family and friends be able to put into words what it was that you lived your life for and what determined the course of your days?

What a shame that we often do more planning ahead for

our vacations than for our lives. On *purpose*, we decide where we would like to go, what we want to take, and map out how to get there. We check on what provisions we might need and pack accordingly. If such great detail is taken for a simple vacation, how much more must we *purpose* to live our life so we don't get off course. We'd better make sure when we get off course that we know right where we're going so we can return to the original chart to make sure we get to our life destination properly.

What's a Woman to Do?

The Lord has a definite plan and purpose for each of us. It is a personal, practical, and perfect plan. What I wrote down in my journal as my number one goal in life over twenty-five years ago still holds true for me. Today, it would be known as my life message:

*I want to live in such a way that my life points others
to love the true and living God.*

Underneath that statement I wrote phrases from a song I'd heard since I was a child:

"Only one life, 'twill soon be past,

Only what's done for Christ will last."

A few years later I added a prayer that Elisabeth Elliot, wife of the martyred missionary Jim Elliot, had copied in her Bible as a young college student. She had recently heard Betty Stam, missionary to China, speak in chapel. I've written it in the front of every new Bible or journal of mine since. You might want to do the same:

"Lord, I give up all my own plans and purposes, my own desires and hopes, and accept THY WILL for my life. I give myself, my all, my life utterly to Thee ... to be Thine forever. Fill me and seal me; where Thou wilt, work out Thine own whole will in my life at any cost, now and forever."

Throughout these many years in my adult life, rewriting and praying to God aloud as I wrote those sentences, I always sign my name and that day's date. I make the closing read:

Signed, AT ANY COST,

Sharon

Those have been meaningful times of recommitment for my heart—going regularly into the secret place where the Lord graciously reveals His plan step by step through His Word. What a privilege it was last year to speak in a conference with Elisabeth Elliott and to have her sign one of my Bibles just under where I had written the prayer she had given as a pattern.

Maybe you'd like to copy down the same life message and prayer. Or create your own. I encourage you to get away for at least one day alone to envision and recapture your own shelved aspirations. Borrow an empty office, rent a motel room, or plant yourself alone on a beach—whatever it takes to give yourself silence and an uninterrupted day of retreat. Listen for the Lord's promptings in your heart. Write them down. Be specific and courageous as you write.

Until I clarified on paper what was important to me, yes, even worth dying for, I never truly knew. Wait until you see it on paper! Putting your longings into words helps you,

define ways you can set out to accomplish
and goals in life. Dreaming and purposing
done hastily.

At least twice a year, I take a personal retreat for twenty-four uninterrupted hours with the Lord. Sincerely seeking God's will and listening to His heart from His Word has dramatically aided my personal and professional ministry. My inner spirit is refueled, and I am repositioned to where I hope to be going and to what I hope to accomplish by the time my life on this earth is ended.

PLANNING YOUR PERSONAL RETREAT

"One of these days I'd like to do that, Sharon," I can almost hear you promising. "But I've got three young children and a full-time job. I'm uncertain how to start ... " your sentence trails off into a long sigh. "Maybe someday...."

Why not now? I have to admit that until I actually made the reservation for my own personal one-day and one-night retreat, I was tempted to back out. I figured I already knew where I stood, what my purpose in life was. And, hey, I could journal all that down sipping a cup of coffee at my own kitchen table. I didn't need to get away.

My first "for real" getaway was actually when I scheduled to stay one extra day in a beautiful resort after speaking at a women's conference (appealing ambience and beauty plays an important part in getting my creative juices flowing). I can hardly describe the powerful effect that this particular twenty-four-hour period had on my life. God nurtured me and loved me as if He was holding me in His loving embrace.

I reflected on His Word; I walked; I practiced and memorized Scripture verses; I reveled in the stimuli of nature sitting on a lone bench outdoors overlooking a beautiful lake. What a deep sense of communication the Father and I enjoyed in prayer. It was as if no one else were there for miles around. I ate my meals alone in my room saturated with praise music.

I want you to envision yourself doing the same. Give yourself permission to be totally absorbed in uninterrupted time with your heavenly Father, talking with Him, immersed in sweet communion. You'll come away filled with more self-discovery and a deeper vulnerability with God after twenty-four straight hours with Him. The Lord longs for this type of intimacy with you!

There are no ground rules. Simply schedule your special day away. Allowing yourself to retreat gives you the critical time you need to reflect and find purpose for your life. By taking time for yourself in such a lavish way, you are saying, "I deserve the same love and care that I give to those I love."

Where will I go? What will I do? Here are some suggestions:

Give yourself permission to comfort yourself. Turn off your inner critic that says, "You shouldn't do this, people are depending on you." A whole weekend isn't necessary, but it's nice. Even an eight-hour workday alone, a Saturday, an afternoon off work—the options are endless. Even if you live alone, it is still best to go to another location to avoid routine and the familiar. Prepare for all household and family needs ahead of time so that you aren't having to call home or be distracted by remembering things during your retreat that you might have left undone. If you live alone, turn on the message machine.

Splurge a little on yourself if at all possible. A little pampering is always a welcome gift to ourselves. Go away to a lovely motel or resort, if possible. (No ugly letters from husbands, please!) An enjoyable, beautiful environment stirs up a loveliness in our souls as women and facilitates those internal ponderings. Even if you live alone, going as far as just across town is beneficial to feeling "away from it all." The place will be different for each of us. One woman might enjoy a horse ranch while another might choose an environment conducive to gardens and waterfalls. To me, my ideal retreat alone would be in a lovely bed and breakfast where I could have meals privately and walk the beach by the ocean. You choose the setting that provides the stimuli that helps you "come away for awhile" as Jesus beckons us to do.

Take very little with you on your getaway. You might want a change of clothing, your Bible and journal, and a maximum of one book other than your Bible (perhaps a devotional). You will need bedclothes and a few toiletries. And I would encourage you to take some flowers (perhaps a rose or freesia), sachet, a praise CD with player, and a fragrant candle. The smaller bag you pack, the better. By taking little, you won't be tempted to primp, organize, or be distracted from the real purpose of your retreat.

IMMERSE YOURSELF IN GOD'S COMFORT

I've heard many women say, "But, once I got away on a personal retreat I wouldn't know what to do or where to start."

Design your day of retreat so that your body, soul, emotions, and mind receive refreshment and renewal. Don't bring a set agenda. Here are a few suggestions that have helped me over the years:

Begin your day by opening your journal to a blank page and write at the top, "In my life I would like to ... " After you've pondered for awhile and written all that comes to your heart, end the page (or pages) with a written prayer to the Lord. Start your prayer with the key sentence that Saul of Tarsus (later known as the apostle Paul) asked of God on the road to Damascus, "Lord, what do You want me to do?" (Acts 9:6 NKJV). Next, pour out your heart's desires, starting, "With God's help, I purpose to _____." I encourage you to end that prayer with the prayer above I had written down from Elisabeth Elliot's example.

Turn the page and title the next page, "What I am most afraid of." (If you get stuck after awhile on the first exercise, go to this one for a time and then back and forth). On this page write out a personal prayer of your fears to the Lord. Please do write them out—in longhand, not on your laptop. There is something about the slowing down of our thinking processes when we put what begins as a thought in our head to a pen in our hand writing on paper. You may find tears streaming down your cheeks like I have as I faced fears. Often, other women have told me they have done the same.

Finally, at the top of another journal page, write, "I am thankful for blessings ... My joy list." Number your paper 1 to 100. This list alone can make your day of retreat one of the most fruitful, rewarding, and satisfying days of your adult life. Before you screech, "But I don't have a hundred things!" hear me out. As I look back to the first time I did this, I began writing one word blessings on each line: family … the Bible … health … my job … my best friend … and on I went. Slowly, I began to cultivate a thankful heart and unexpected blessings began to pop into my head. I became aware of how much in my life I really did have! Almost two hours later I had filled in my 100 lines, but didn't stop there. My list kept growing and before I knew it, my prayers that followed were full of praise, not my problems.

What a gift you will be giving yourself!

MAKING A DIFFERENCE

Do I sound preachy? Perhaps it is because I am talking loudest to myself. That eighty-fifth birthday will be here before I know it! There is no better time for me (and you) to assess the values that are worthy of my time and effort for the second half of my life. At eighty-five, I must look back on something more meaningful than houses or property, clothes, or stocks and bonds.

We would do well to note what author Madeleine L'Engle wrote in her journal:

> I have to try, but I do not have to succeed. Following Christ has nothing to do with success. It has to do with love. During the ten years when practically nothing I wrote was published, I was as much a writer … as I am now; it may happen that there will come another time when I can't find anyone to publish my

work. If this happens, it won't matter. It will hurt. But, I did learn ... that success is not my motivation.[2]

Nothing else matters in this life if I do not find and fulfill the purpose for which God created me. Success, fame, and fortune are to no avail if others cannot recall a consistent life serving the God who saved me, a loving family, and an earnest attempt to invest in the lives of others.

ESTHER: A WOMAN FOR HER TIMES

About 485 years before the birth of Christ the Jewish nation was struggling for a humble existence after being taken captive in the land of Persia. In these desperate circumstances God used a beautiful and quiet Jewish orphan girl to save His chosen nation from sure ruin. Her story has been recorded in the book graced by her name. Esther was her Persian name and meant "star." Surely she was a bright star in the history of women everywhere.

King Ahasuerus determined to find the most beautiful girl in the land to be his queen. Surprisingly, Esther was chosen as one of the finalists. Then, in this remarkable beauty contest, this quiet Jewish girl became the queen. Her life was forever changed. Instead of toiling as a captive Jew in exile, she would have the wealth and luxury that only royalty of that day enjoyed. As queen, everything she wanted was hers for the asking.

But God had other plans for this faithful woman. She learned of a subtle plot that would mean the annihilation of the Jewish people in Persia. In order to bring an end to this terrible plan, Esther would have to risk her life. But there was more to this woman than drop-dead gorgeous looks and a glittering wardrobe. In a plot that would rival any thriller of our day, she developed a scheme that would save her nation. But there was one hitch. The honor code of the Persians stated that if you appeared before the king without an invitation and were rejected, you were to be put to death. Esther understood that by intervening she might die, and simply said, "If I perish, I perish!" It wasn't that she didn't value her life, but she realized an important principle that we all must realize: some things are more important in this life than life itself. Of course Esther understood the consequences. She was the queen—she knew the rules well. But Esther, you see, knew that there were some things more important than her own existence. In challenging her to action, her cousin Mordecai spoke words of encouragement that have challenged great men and women to this very day. "For if you remain silent at this time, relief and deliverance for the Jews will arise from another place, but you and your father's family will perish. And who knows but that you have come to royal position for such a time as this?" (Esth. 4:14).

History reveals that Esther did not remain quiet. She took the risk that could have cost her life. In doing so, her life was spared, and her nation. Because this GIFTed woman chose to *purpose* in her heart to make a difference in the lives around her, a nation's history was continued, and her name is honored among women of the world.

This quiet little Hebrew girl did her part in opening the way for the coming of the world's Savior. Like many today,

God had her hidden away for *His purpose*. When the day came, God brought her to the forefront to work out His plan. Esther made up her mind to make a difference in her world even at the cost of her own life if necessary. Esther stands out as God's chosen vessel; this sweet, willing Hebrew girl was brought to the kingdom "for such a time as this."

What wonderful plans might our gracious and loving God have for you? What place of influence might He want you to pursue with purpose? More important, what might happen if you chose not to accept God's purpose for your life? Who might not reach their God-chosen potential because you prefer to take life's easy road and not purpose in your heart to be a GIFTed woman?

TWO PICTURES DECADES APART

Not long ago Rob and I were borrowing some friends' house while they wintered in Arizona. We were between ministries and had already sold our home. We lived in Lois and Chuck's house for only four months. During this time there were important lessons to be learned, starting on the very first morning.

The utter brevity of time on this planet was dramatically emphasized during my devotional time that first day. It felt strange living in someone else's home, so I hoped my morning routine would help me feel more at home. I read awhile, prayed awhile, journaled, sipped coffee—all my usual devotional procedure. Looking around the room while pondering some Scripture verses aloud, I was struck by two framed photographs. Sitting atop the piano in a corner was a color picture of a quite elderly woman obviously dressed up for the photo session. Directly across the room on a small table at the end of the couch sat a black and white picture of a handsome, young couple in turn-of-the-century wedding attire.

I couldn't help but stare at one and then the other. The eyes and smile and tilt of the head of the women in both prints appeared to be identical. Was it the same woman? Later in the week, I asked. Pleased to find out that they were, I visually learned to appreciate how swiftly time passes. During desperate days and nights when Rob and I struggled in prayer for God's leading in a future ministry, I often felt like giving up. Sometimes I saw utterly no hope of ever being relocated and moved out by our May deadline when Lois and Chuck would need their home again.

But each morning and often through my days, the message of those two photographs filled me with the extra courage I needed to persevere. Sitting at opposite ends of a living room, they represented over fifty years of time. How quickly life passes. And I did not want the span of time between two photographs of me someday to be full of wasted, empty years. It was a turning point, one of those incredible moments when the heavens seem to open up and fill my heart with confidence and hope.

Take a good look at your life. And note the closing words of Romans 8:28: "… those who … are called according to his purpose" (NLT). Because you are one of His special "called ones," I urge you to *purpose* to let God fulfill His purpose in you. Allow Queen Esther to be your example and Christ to be your strength. God doesn't ask us to understand each of the events that take place in our life, only to trust that He is working His purpose in us.

That takes courage. I think of so many women I know who encourage me onward as I have purposed to live the rest of my life with eternity's values. Their lives are godly influences that I can imitate. A long time ago these godly mentors quit trying to please other people and made up their minds that what really mattered was pleasing the Lord. I have not heard one of them say that they wished they'd spent more time in their office working, or scrubbing floors, or buying more stylish outfits. All have encouraged me to live by faith, not by sight. It's a wonderful way to live—looking forward to hearing, *"Well done, my good and faithful servant."* There's no doubt about it—it's an exciting time to be a woman serving the Lord! This favorite quote of mine from Dr. James Dobson sits on my desk. It says what I want to say so well:

I have concluded that the accumulation of wealth, even if I could achieve it, is an insufficient reason for living. When I reach the end of my days, a moment or two from now, I must look backward on something more meaningful than the pursuit of houses and land and machines and stocks and bonds.

Nor is fame of any lasting benefit. I will consider my earthly existence to have been wasted unless I can recall a loving family, consistent investment in the lives of people, and an earnest attempt to serve God who made me. *Nothing else matters.*[3]

Living in light of eternity, one life becomes a GIFT that touches another, that touches another, that touches another, and another....

SECRET Three

PRECIOUS ACCEPTANCE

∞

A GIFTed woman finds PRECIOUS ACCEPTANCE
and value in Jesus Christ.

Be healed and held by the Savior.

After finding and sitting in my assigned seat on the exit
row I reached for the mail I'd stuffed in my briefcase as I left
for a weekend conference. I was not prepared for the shock
I felt as I read the words in the first letter I opened:

Dear Sharon,

I've tried to tell you before, but chickened out.
Now I must tell someone.

I'm losing the battle. I try to be happy, but I'm not.
The empty void in my heart is still just as empty.
I have no purpose. I can't find my way.

I can't do this anymore.

I'm unbearably alone.

Now I have thoughts I never dreamed I would have—SUICIDE.

On a plane several thousand feet above the ground, there was nothing I could do but pray. And that's exactly what I did! I had heard about other women in similar crises and all too often no one knew about it until it was too late. My imagination began running wild. *What if… ?*

I didn't know it at the time, but that letter became the catalyst for the direction my life was to take in the coming years. To whom could women go for direction? Who could define our identity as women running headlong into a brand-new century? I was confronted in a very personal way with the devastating uncertainty of worth in the hearts of many, many women.

I felt like I had to do my part. I wanted to speak face to face with my friend who had penned those words from her hurting heart. I wanted to tell her that Christ truly can give her everything she was longing for and searching for and so much more.

I wanted to love her, put my arms around her slumping shoulders, and tell her that I know the way out of her pain. I do know the Way. It is through Jesus Christ, who said, "I am the way, the truth, and the life" (John 14:6 NLT). I longed to share with her that she doesn't ever have to be alone again for Jesus promises that when you are His own, He will *"never leave you or forsake you"* (Heb. 13:5 NRSV, emphasis added).

I was compelled to encourage this dear one to trade all

her anger, shame, grief, disappointment, self-hate, and hopelessness for God's extravagant love. He longed to lavish His love upon her. It's the only joyful and liberating way to live! Living in the preciousness of God makes everything different—every one of us is a special creation of God. Deep joy comes from knowing that we do not have to depend on the reactions of others or our desperate circumstances to determine how we will live from day to day.

I ran straight to a pay phone when my plane touched down in the next city. I called a friend who immediately threw herself into her car and drove straight to the letter writer's home. Later in the weekend I returned to find quite a contrast! I found the beginning hints of joy on this woman's face, so different from the desperate words I'd read in her letter. My eyes filled with tears as I listened to her tell the whole story about overwhelming heartache and misery she had experienced in recent years. As I quietly listened, her sad story made sense. No wonder she was filled with deep grief that drained her of any sense of hope.

No Wonder She Changed

"I have loved you with an everlasting love; I have drawn you with loving-kindness" (Jer. 31:3). The troubled woman found these words to be the key to help her grasp how precious she is to God. Scripture calmed her anxious heart when her father had rejected her. Her daddy had suddenly decided he did not want her in his life. He told her he had "no love in his heart for her anymore." Being excluded from a parent like that was devastating. She desperately needed to know that God loves her; that He longs to enter into an intimate relationship with her; and that He is waiting patiently for her to run to Him.

Maybe you, like me, need to be reminded of those truths today. My heavenly Father is patiently waiting for you to come to Him. His arms are not crossed in a symbol of unconcern. They are wide open. One of the most precious pictures of personal peace is of a baby sleeping in his mother's arms. Rocking gently, the baby no longer squirms, but rests quietly as an early spring snowflake cradled in a beautiful spring flower. You can't tell who enjoys the serenity more, the mother or her child. A deep mellow contentment wells up into my heart every time I see that sight. The prophet Zephaniah describes a similar emotion in the heart of God. "The Lord your God is with you, he is mighty to save. He will take great delight in you, he will quiet you with his love, he will rejoice over you with singing" (Zeph. 3:17).

Nestle up to Jesus today. He's waiting for you. He will not cast you away. In the Hebrew text, the word "love" in this verse is in the feminine form as a declaration, "I have loved thee with an everlasting Mother-love." The picture is that of a mother and her children. It speaks of the pampering, tender, nurturing character of God. There has never been another baby born like you and there never will be. Every detail right down to your DNA has meticulously been imagined, then created by God. And today, every detail of your life is an indication of God's love for you. Henry Blackaby states this in such a beautiful way.

No matter what the circumstances are, His love never changes. The cross, the death of Jesus Christ, and His resurrection are God's final, total, and complete expression that He loves us.... He created you for that love relationship. He has been pursuing you in that love relationship. Every dealing he has with you is an expression of His love for you. God would cease to be God if He expressed Himself in any other way than *perfect love*.[4]

Even though there are over five billion people on this planet, your molecular structure is all your own. Imagine that—only God could think up that many variations. Your heavenly Father has been with you all the way.

Oh, such love! I suggest today that we must look only to the Lord and not at people, problems, and circumstances around us. You can bring every little care and every emergency case to Him, for He loves and cares for you (1 Peter 5:7). Even in the face of Calvary, dying for the sinful world, love was His response to a jeering, mocking crowd. Eagerly and joyfully receive His message of love for you today, dear one.

Do I write to you today? You who may be in the valley of discouragement? You don't *look like* the standard Proverbs 31 woman? You don't *sound like* everyone else? You don't *act like* others who fit the mold? Perhaps you have been rejected and are about to pen words in a letter like the one I received.

Look closely—see the demonstrated love of One whose expressed goal for creating us is to love us. See how precious to God you are. The Bible reveals God's total interest in you as an individual person. The psalmist described in one of his most beautiful prayers, "I praise you because I am fearfully and wonderfully made; your works are wonderful, I know that full well" (Ps. 139:14). You can be *you*. Believe what God's Word tells you about yourself and about His love for you. Find your identity in Him. Not in performance, power, possession, or popularity.

When we trust in Jesus Christ and let Him put our lives together: "For we are God's workmanship, created in Christ Jesus" (Eph. 2:10). Could anyone be more precious than that? There's only one you—the mold has been broken. God put a lot of thought into making each one of us unique. I love thinking on that—picturing God Himself personally prescribing my every detail in His mind. The psalmist also declared, "How precious to me are your thoughts, O God! How vast is the sum of them!" (Ps. 139:17).

If I read that correctly, we did not "just happen." God loves us each so much that He arranged every detail of my being and is involved in everyday specifics from the moment of my conception. Then, God loved whom He created so much that He gave His only Son for me. He considers each one of us important enough to do that! He feels our pain; He shares our sorrows; He loves unconditionally. Hallelujah! No wonder we can entrust our very life into His care!

An illustration that I heard as a little girl brings this into focus. I heard an elderly pastor at summer camp tell about Niagara Falls. He had been there and challenged us to pretend we were standing near the beautiful, yet dangerous falls. Suppose a circus performer strung a rope across the falls to push a wheelbarrow on it to the other side. If he lost his balance, he would fall to the crushing waters below. Just before he starts, the stuntman turns to the bystanders and asks, "Do you think I can do it?"

I remember the old preacher asked us kids the question and we roared, "Yeeeees!" Then he told how the stuntman went on to say, "If you really believe I can do it, who wants to get in with me?" That kind of trust in God takes our relationship with Him further than simply believing He has the power to create us. It involves risk to depend upon Him, even when it is tough. Yes, it is getting into the wheelbarrow, knowing the journey at times might be perilous across deep waters. You are so precious to God that He will never let you go! You are not insignificant to Him. Too many women never begin to do what God intended them to do because they cannot grasp the unconditional love of their Father.

You are a new creation in Christ Jesus—not a rebuilt good-for-nothing. He calls you beloved; His "friend" (John 15:15). You were created for His glory, precious in His sight, chosen, and held by His right hand. These tender expressions of His love are found in Isaiah 43. Oh, how I love that whole chapter! Full of esteem-building confidence to face whatever bogs you down.

That's what my dear friend began to see. When was the last time someone called you "precious"? Lift your little chin up to Jesus. Imagine Him holding it softly between His two nail-scarred hands and calling you His "precious." Perhaps no one has ever cherished and valued you like that before. Imagining such tenderness may even feel a bit uncomfortable to you. I can only tell you that, regardless of apparent failures and discouragements, I cannot begin my day unless I first affirm His love for me through His Word.

No Unimportant People Here

Let Christ satisfy your soul-hunger. There's only one you. Start today to enjoy being you!

God is the only One who truly values us all the time and can create a sense of worth in us. He promises in Philippians 1:6 (NASB) "that He who began a good work in you will perfect it until the day of Christ Jesus." When you came to Him in salvation, He began a work; and He *is* going to complete that work. He's painting a masterpiece of your life. He wants you to be the best you that you can possibly be. He knows what it will take for you to be just that. He knows, also, what it will take for you to look like Him. He's willing to take a lifetime to create a lovely masterpiece. You're that important to Him. He loves you that dearly.

"Give thanks to the LORD, call on his name; make known among the nations what he has done. Sing to him, sing praise to him; tell of all his wonderful acts" (Ps. 105:1–2). You are His wondrous work! Are you afraid of God as your Father? Are you afraid that He might reject, punish, or shame you? Some women (and men) get so down on themselves that they start to think God could never cherish them. Accepting God's love can be particularly difficult for the woman whose relationship with her earthly father was difficult.

I hear from many women at conferences all across our

land who struggle with their God-as-my-Father relationship—especially if they were raised in an abusive family where the father violated body, mind, and soul. What's so sad is that it makes natural sense from a human standpoint. As one woman told me, "It's so hard for me to love God since He is a man. I emotionally and physically sold out to my father. His harsh attacks were so strong that I let him dominate my life. It's hard for me to relate to any man."

No matter how old you are, your relationship with your earthly father has had a major impact on the person you are and the relationship you have today with your heavenly Father. Here are some thoughts along this premise to consider:

• **IF** your father was an unforgiving, harsh authoritarian, you are probably not going to see God as a forgiving, accepting, loving heavenly Father.

• **IF** your dad was an absentee father, there might be a tendency for you to feel like God isn't really interested in you either.

• **IF** your dad responded like you were "in the way" of his agenda, you might be particularly hesitant to bring your cares, and concerns, and questions before almighty God. After all, He has the whole world to think about.

• **IF** you felt guilty or disgraced for developing into a young woman around your daddy, you will probably have a terrible time risking and being vulnerable with God.

• **IF** your father was extremely critical and you felt like you could never please him, you are probably fearful of never pleasing God.

• **IF** you were punished severely by your father for defeats or disobeying him, you may feel like God has certain rules and regulations that you must always attain for Him to accept you.

• **IF** you were abused by your earthly father or stepfather or any male, you may live in a hopeless helplessness and in disgrace before God. It may be difficult to believe that God has not done a terrible injustice in your life.

• **IF** your daddy declared you a label such as a "mistake" or "failure," you may develop self-destructive thoughts and habits and assume that God made His first mistake when He made you.

• **IF** your daddy left the home, divorced your mother, or deserted your family when you were young, you may fear abandonment. It may be tough to believe that God says He will never leave you nor forsake you.

Do you identify with any of the above statements? Go to God with it; He understands. Read aloud to Him in prayer the statement(s) that you feel apply to your current relationship with God. Ask God to reveal to you any distorted concepts. Seek to see God as a heavenly parent very different from your earthly parents. Use your personal journal to record your observations. Begin now! Replace your previous negative perceptions with the truth about God, your Father. He's amazing! It's about time you had the joy of discovering the truth about yourself—that you *are precious.* For too long you have struggled with feelings of being alienated from God due to underlying pain from your past. You can be set free from the cycle of rejection and failure. It's time you told yourself the truth about your heavenly Father—claiming victory over the lies the enemy wants you to believe. As always, we have to recognize there is a problem before we seek to change it.

The more I hear the cries of women raised by abusive, rigid fathers, the more I see how it affects their intimacy with God. Likewise, I thank God for the godly father I am privileged to still have on this earth. Daddy has been one of the very few constants I have had throughout my entire life. I guess that's why it is so easy for me to accept that my heavenly Father never leaves me nor forsakes me. My daddy did the best he knew to do after my mother passed away; I do not take his care during that time for granted. He could have shipped my sister and me off somewhere and gotten on with the rest of his life. I'm sure there were those who encouraged him to. I'm glad he did not, for God used his parental instinct to show me many aspects of God's fatherliness.

As a child I was abandoned by my birth mother— through no choosing of her own. I barely knew her, but do have a few memories of her. Death took her when I was only three years old. This was in the early 1950s when tuberculosis and polio were serious killer diseases. My mama contracted both.

If I didn't admit that I'm sorry that I never got to really know my birth mother, I'd not be telling the truth. Most of the bond I share with her has been gained through her journals and what family has shared with me. What I honestly regret even more, however, is the way I held my new mother at arm's length for so long. We have enjoyed as close of a loving mother-daughter relationship as can be since my mid-twenties. We are cherished friends. We can talk freely about the past—even laugh at my actions as a young girl when I used to be such a brat. (I would stick out my tongue at Mother and do other naughty actions to try to get her not to care for me.)

Mother and I now both give God all the glory for His power to redeem pain and transform relationships. But when Daddy remarried two years after my mama's death, I was afraid to get close to my new mother. After all, look at all the dear women who helped out with my care during my mama's illnesses or after she died. I was either taken from them and not allowed to stay at their home very long, or they died on me! So all my growing up years, I alienated people by being ugly to them. I reasoned, "It might hurt less if I reject them first." I unconsciously sabotaged relationships because I had grown so used to living in a world of uncertainty.

Daily I am amazed by the grace of God. When I write about not measuring up and insecurity, believe me, I know what I'm talking about. Even now, I'm blinking back tears as I write. I am so thankful for healing and am overwhelmed with God's grace and power. I haven't arrived; I haven't always felt precious; but I have developed a pretty healthy self-image because of God's love and fathering of me. He has parented me all these years. He has taught me that my identity is not in *who* I am, but in *whose* I am. It is what psychologists call "noncontingent love"—that is, its presence does not depend on our loving in return or behaving in a particular way. It is a part of God's parenthood—we are His children, so He loves us. Period.

THE SECRET WEAPON GOD USES

My own parent-shaped misperceptions of God created some struggles in my relationship with Him until I began to learn what God's character is really like. My pursuit of knowing God better began by my becoming more childlike in my posture toward Him. He knows we all need the warmth and closeness that He can give us best as a caring Father. He can "father me" only when I am willing to "become as a little child," crawl up in His lap, and become His little girl. I was challenged to do a biblical search on the attributes of God. The Bible revealed so many trusting, reliable truths about God's character. That was the secret weapon to opening up a whole new parent-child intimacy between us. Coming to God as a child is a state of mind, a posture I voluntarily took. He wasn't going to leave me, abandon me, or die on me. God keeps His promises. He is here to stay.

My heavenly Father is loving, kind, and patient.
My heavenly Father is not quick to criticize.
My heavenly Father is longsuffering and holy.

My heavenly Father is righteous—always good.

My heavenly Father delights in me.

My heavenly Father is not arrogant.

My heavenly Father is reliable, always the same, never changing.

My heavenly Father is with me everywhere I go.

My heavenly Father does not gloat when I sin and fail.

My heavenly Father has no beginning and no end.

My heavenly Father is fair, just, and consistent.

To some degree, I had spent my entire childhood and teen years afraid that my Daddy or Mother would leave or die. Then, after marrying Rob, I projected that same fear toward him. To complicate matters, as I've mentioned, I waited far too long to trust the mother who raised me. As any adoptee knows, she may not have given me birth, but she's my mother. My insatiable need to feel loved and secure was only fulfilled when I stopped looking to significant people in my life to define my identity and fulfill my needs. It came when I based it solely upon God's love. It's been a long journey throughout my entire adult life and there have been temporary setbacks. Defining the problem was part of finding the solution. That solution came when I accepted God's love for me as His child. Read this paraphrase of 1 Corinthians 13 aloud to yourself today and every morning for a month. Then see how your feelings about yourself and your Father have changed:

Because God loves me, He is slow to lose patience with me.

Because God loves me, He takes the circumstances of my life and uses them in a constructive way for my growth.

Because God loves me, He does not treat me as an object to be possessed and manipulated.

Because God loves me, He has no need to impress me with how great and powerful He is because He is God. Nor does He belittle me as His child in order to show me how important He is.

Because God loves me He is for me, He wants to see me mature and develop in His love.

Because God loves me, He does not send down His wrath on every little mistake I make—of which there are many.

Because God loves me, He does not keep score of all my sins and then beat me over the head with them whenever He gets a chance.

Because God loves me, He is deeply grieved when I do not walk in the ways that please Him because He sees this as evidence that I don't trust Him and love Him as I should.

Because God loves me, He keeps working patiently with me even when I feel like giving up and can't see why He doesn't give up on me too.

Because God loves me, He keeps on trusting me, even at times when I don't trust myself.

Because God loves me, He never says there is no hope for me, rather, He patiently works with me, loves me, and disciplines me in such a way that it is hard for me to understand the depth of His concern for me.

Because God loves me, He never forsakes me even though many of my friends (or family) might.[5]

ABBA, FATHER

Most Christians struggle with the effects of the past or present relationships to some degree. Don't let Satan rob you of the preciousness of a tender Father-child relationship with God. Satan is a liar and a thief and if you let him, he will rob you of everything you hold dear. For you precious ones who endured blatant abuse or injury as unjust as incest, my hand and heart goes out to you. I don't pretend to lump my abandonment issues with something as devastating as victimization, but we can both hold the same verse dear in our hearts, "I can do everything through him who gives me strength" (Phil. 4:13).

Sandra Wilson, Ph.D. and therapist, struggled for years with her own pain as an incest survivor. It wasn't until she became a Christian in her early teens that she began to know the sweetness of a trusting Father relationship.

God is angry about the abuse you endured as a child. I invite you to consider re-examining the scene of your abuse from God's perspective. *God knows it was not your fault, no matter what your abuser told you!* If you have never tried to look at your abuse this way, you might want to find a trusted friend, a pastor, or a counselor who could provide support and comfort as you experience the anger, sadness, and other feelings that might emerge.

Please remember, you will not feel these emotions with such overwhelming intensity forever. Giving yourself permission to cry, shout, talk, and write them out seems to help.[6]

Now that I've told you my story, what is yours? Continue to let God mend you. Don't claim Scarlett O'Hara's famous line, "I'll just think about that tomorrow!"

Go to your Father. You're in good company. As Jesus did in the Garden of Gethsemane the night before the cross, address your heavenly Father, as *Abba*, the Aramaic term for "Daddy," the familiar, childlike name for "father." Let Him cherish you. God has always been in the business of reconstructing lives. Abandon the idea that you have to be a self-sufficient adult and become a schoolgirl again. Sit at the feet of your Father and, like a child, learn about the kingdom afresh and anew. Don't flunk the test of childhood like the rich young ruler in the Bible. He apparently could not make the humbling descent into childhood, because the Bible says, "he went away sad" (Mark 10:22).

Look at a couple of places where Paul talks about God as father. "Those who are led by the Spirit of God are sons of God" (Rom. 8:14). "Because you are sons, God sent the Spirit of his Son into our hearts, the Spirit who calls out, *Abba*, Father" (Gal. 4:6). A literal rendering of the terms "Abba, Father" would read, Beloved Daddy—a very real, very near, very tender personal father. Even in those times when you can't feel like He is near, God is near. You are not facing your pain alone. It comes down to trusting. Just like a little child.

YOUR BEAUTIFUL METAMORPHOSIS

Several years ago during a particularly difficult time, I recorded my feelings every day in my journal. Anger. Sadness. Joy. I pondered each emotion as I prayed and read the Bible. Then I gathered verses to pray that matched each of my varied feelings. They all had one common denominator—each verse proved to be an antidote for my emotions.

The list became a real part of my everyday living. For weeks I memorized and meditated upon a specific *fact* when I encountered that particular personal negative *feeling*. Sometimes I even said aloud "STOP!" to remind myself not to give in to feelings, but take hold of a biblical fact. Jesus, God's own Son, repeatedly responded with Scripture when the devil tempted Him in the wilderness (Matt. 4). Jesus is the pattern we are to follow—to "hide the Word in our heart" that we might resist when taunted by the evil one.

Whoa! A metamorphosis of my mind took place in my head that trickled all the way down into my heart. God used these verses to say, "Sharon, I lovingly want to replace and satisfy all that deep hunger in your soul. I long to become Who and What you've longed for, for so long. Only as you receive Me to fill your dry, empty soul, will you truly be filled to overflowing."

Even today, despite speaking often in front of large audiences, I can feel strangely insecure or out-of-place in a room full of people at times. I still am afraid of rejection and want to appear in control of my life. I suspect that pride motivates me at times. But understanding that deep root of abandonment from my childhood and that it will still at times emerge, I know to take my fears and humiliation to the Lord. I carry these verses (and many more) on 3 x 5 note cards and lambaste the enemy with them. I recite them and undergo my own form of brainwashing—giving my mind a bath!

I admit I haven't completely conquered my insecurities … but they no longer are conquering me. I am spending more time at the feet of my Abba Father and growing more deeply in love with Him as I do. I believe it has helped me move from living a sluggish caterpillar existence into enjoying a beautiful butterfly level of life!

MY FEELINGS	GOD'S FACTS
Worry	Cast all my care upon Him, He cares for me. 1 Peter 5:7
Guilt	God will forgive me. 1 John 1:9; Romans 8:1
Fear	He has not given me a spirit of fear. 1 Timothy 1:7
Anger at circumstances I can't change	God is for me—working things for my good. Romans 28–31
Frustrated at not seeing a plan	God has a plan. Jeremiah 29:11; Proverbs 16:3

Selfish desires	Conform to His will—it is best. Romans 12:1–2
Proud, self-sufficient	God gives grace to the humble. James 4:6
Insecurity	God knows His sheep. I can't be plucked away. John 10:27–29
Hopeless	God will be my fortress. Psalm 62:5–8
Unloved	Nothing can separate me from God's love. Psalm 36:7–10; Romans 8:38–39
Defeat	God can give me victory. Ephesians 4:27
Brokenhearted	God is close to me when I'm crushed in my spirit. Psalm 43:18
Not knowing what to pray	The Holy Spirit will pray for me. Romans 8:26–27
Troubled	I don't need to let my heart be troubled. John 14:1–3
Tearful	God will help me reap in joy. Psalm 126:3, 5–6
Abandoned	God will hold me safe—no terror can reach me. Ps 91:1, 4–5,

9–11

Defeated	God defeats all adversaries. Psalm 92:14–15
Weak	God reigns forever! Psalm 97:1, 3, 6
Alone in battle	God is my helper. Psalm 118:5–7
Unloving	God is love. 1 John 4:8
Defeated by the enemy	God has overcome the world. Satan has no hold on me. John 14:30
Losing ground	God will help me stand my ground. Ephesians 6:14–16
Last in comparison	God accepts me. 2 Corinthians 10:12
Forgotten	God never forgets about me. Isaiah 49:15
Fear from failing strength	God will uphold me. Isaiah 41:10
Lack comfort	God is able to comfort me. 2 Corinthians 1:3–5
Depressed	God is my hope, joy, and peace. Psalm 62:5–6
Not handling change	God never changes. Malachi 3:6

For every need, God provides a promise and a blessing. Remember, there is nothing you can do to earn the love and acceptance of God—that's the nature of God. He has no trouble seeing past our flaws and weaknesses of today; for He sees what we are going to be tomorrow.

THERE'S A LITTLE GIRL IN EVERY WOMAN

A healthy attitude toward our precious-ness begins when we accept that there is far more to self-worth than shape, size, or outer appearance. It's much more than power and prestige or popularity. It's about knowing more of our God as "Abba, Daddy;" it's not so much learning more about ourselves.

Imagine a little seven-year-old girl who has only known pain and rejection from her father whom she loves dearly here on this earth. But she knows that to him, she will never be good enough, quiet enough, pretty enough. At Sunday school when she is taught that God is her heavenly Father, what is she going to perceive? There's only one answer to that question. She doesn't need to know more about herself; she needs to learn more about God and His sweet love for her—unconditionally.

There's a bit of that little girl inside every grown woman. When I was a little girl I played dress-up, rocked dolls, swung as high as the treetops, and had the best adventures riding my bike. I admit, now that I'm fifty, there are days I would love to trade my adult responsibilities and become that carefree little girl again.

Popsicles … summer camp … sand boxes … drawing with crayons … slamming the screen door … gingerly being carried to my bed. I especially liked that. It's a childhood sensation that still resonates in my memory after all these years. You see, it didn't take long to learn that if I was asleep when my family arrived home from church or a trip, my daddy would carefully slide me out of the back seat of the car and carry me to my bed. It is difficult now to recall those tender moments without tears blinding my eyes. They echo in my memory as some of the first messages I received from Daddy—revealing a portrait of what God, my Father, wants to do for me.

Makes me wish I was a little girl again. I can only envision as I close my eyes what it felt like to be carried softly, tenderly in those safe, strong arms. I have a vivid image of Mother looking over her shoulder from the front seat whispering, "Sharon is asleep." Truth be told, I "played possum" more times than not. Didn't matter. Soon I felt Daddy's arms wrapped around me. I'd turn and lean in close to him. Before long, I was cushioned in my own bed. Safe. Secure. Dreaming sweet dreams.

Living far away from my daddy now, I've discovered that same sweet fellowship and security is available to me as a grown woman through God's loving presence. I open up my heart to Him often. Sometimes I run to him with a runny nose on my freckled face and with tear-stained, puffy eyes. When I lean close to Him, He embraces me, carries me, and all sorrow is eased. Sweet dreams.

You can search high and low for that kind of love, but when you have the love of God, your Father, you have all you need. If this chapter has helped you to know anew how precious you are to your loving Father, then the pages have done what I prayed they might do. I do hope you know how very precious you are. Run to your Abba-Daddy today. Lean in close. When you do, you'll find that He's right there beside you, lifting you, gathering you into His arms. Hear Him whisper in *your* ear, "My daughter, you are precious to Me." Sweet dreams.

Four

PRAYER

A GIFTed woman cultivates the private practice of PRAYER.

Influence in public begins with intimacy in private!

Okay, I've been hood-winked; I admit it. I tend to like everything in my house to be perfect and in order (I can hear my family wailing ... "Tend to? Helloooo!"). So I confess; if things aren't the way I think they should be I step in and fix them. Whether it's the magazines on the coffee table, the condiments in the cupboard, or the pillows on the sofa, I am an avowed perfectionist. To the point of being obnoxious, I want things done right. It's really not a pretty picture, is it?

Perhaps you are like me. How often we find ourselves sidetracked by the small things in life at the price of what should be our priorities. Take today, for instance. I wanted, in fact I intended, the day to begin with a quiet, personal moment of intimacy with my best friend. With coffee mug in hand I enthusiastically began to move toward my Bible and prayer journal lying on the pink-flowered, overstuffed chair. But something all too familiar happened.

As I set the coffee down and began to kneel, I eyed a nasty spot of mud on the carpet. Already I was beguiled, fooled into swapping the most important relationship in my life for that little, insignificant token of mud. I am ashamed to say that my kneeling turned into something resembling a curtsy as I reached for something to clean the carpet. How incredibly brazen of me; how could I have let *dried up dirt* seem more pressing than my appointment with God?

Egg-citing Lessons in Prayer

After vacuuming the muddy areas, one thing led to another. *Why stop now?* Before I knew it I'd let myself extend this cleaning frenzy down the upstairs hallway and into two bedrooms. *After all,* I reasoned, *then I won't have to drag the vacuum cleaner out later.* Two phone calls and several other interruptions later and with my stomach growling audibly, I reached for a skillet to scramble some eggs.

By now my mood was anything but pleasant. *I'll never finish the things I need to get done today.* Muttering and growling, I jerked open the blue Styrofoam container in our fridge marked "Grade A Jumbo Eggs."

And there it was, on the inside of the carton lid, of all things, a verse of scripture printed in an elegant font and framed by lovely flowers. "This is the day the LORD has made. We will rejoice and be glad in it" (Ps. 118:24 NLT). I could feel the uncomfortable sting of conviction well up in me like a huge gulp of bitter medicine. I would never have supposed that an egg carton could have given me such a benefit. God's Word is always a valuable gift, no matter what it's printed on. Proving once again His love for me, God graciously chose to use a blue egg carton to remind me that He longs to fellowship with me.

I immediately responded with a quiet prayer. *You're right, Lord. Lately I've been running on empty. With only about two minutes of devotional reading and prayer a day, no wonder I'm so disconnected. How I've missed my time in Your presence.*

THE KEYS TO POWER-PACKED INFLUENCE

It is to our benefit to set aside time to "rejoice and be glad" with Christ. By making it a priority to refresh our spirits daily, to refuel and rejuvenate our souls, and yes, to rejoice with Him in our blessings, we deepen and strengthen our relationships with Him.

Eleven years ago I became firmly convinced that for a woman to make an impact on her world she must make time in her busy routine to know God as her loving Friend and Father. She must set aside uninterrupted time to have two-way conversations with God through prayer and Bible study.

A wise mentor of mine once asked me, "Sharon, where do you want to be and what kind of woman do you want to be in ten years when you turn fifty?" It was, perhaps, the single most important question I have ever been asked. She went on to remind me that if I want to see what I will be like in ten years, I can look at the books I read and the people with whom I spend the most time now. Not knowing how to answer her offhand, I decided to compile a list.

"Ideally," I eventually answered her question, "I want to be more like Jesus. Yes, that's what I want to be like in ten years."

I had no sooner expressed my heart's desire aloud, than I realized that if I truly meant my answer, I would need to make a difficult decision. If it is true that who I am in ten years depends on who I'm with the most and what I read, then I'd better spend time with the One I long to be like. I determined to spend quality time with Jesus.

SIMPLE CHOICES, INCREDIBLE RESULTS!

In life, we all do what we choose to do. To say we don't have time for Christ is to admit that we have placed another voice before His. If we are to be like Christ and allow His power in our lives to influence others, then our relationship with Him must come first. In studying the outstanding women of the Bible, you will find that their relationships with God took priority over every other thing. This relationship of love allowed them to focus and make an impact on everyone around them.

No two women symbolize this principle in the New Testament more than Mary and her sister, Martha. These two early believers were often found in the presence of Jesus and the other disciples. They both demonstrated a love for Christ and a commitment to His purpose. Yet, in a remarkably short passage found in the Gospel of Luke we begin to see a major difference between the two that may be insightful for our topic at hand.

As Jesus and the disciples continued on their way to Jerusalem, they came to a village where a woman named Martha welcomed them into her home. Her sister, Mary, sat at the Lord's feet, listening to what he taught. But Martha was worrying over the big dinner she was preparing. She came to Jesus and said, "Lord, doesn't it seem unfair to you that my sister just sits here while I do all the work? Tell her to come and help me." But the Lord said to her, "My dear Martha, you are so upset over all these details! There is really only one thing worth being concerned about. Mary has discovered it—and I won't take it away from her." (Luke 10:38–42 NLT)

Did you notice the sharp contrast between these two lovely sisters? Martha was *"worried over the big dinner she was preparing,"* while Mary had discovered the one thing to be concerned about. And what was that "one thing"? She was bowing at the feet of her Master.

I don't know about you, but I can relate to Martha's disposition. Doesn't it seem to you that our responsibilities are endless? From routine housework and civic responsibilities, to duties as a mom, to responsibilities in the workplace and at church—we can truly become stressed out and too busy for our own good. The text makes it clear that there is nothing wrong with serving. It is good and proper and necessary. But as with Mary, our relationship with Jesus must come first.

The principle of Luke 10 is this: Our serving should never come at the cost of our relationship with the Savior. Mary's ability to sit at Jesus' feet in spite of her hectic surroundings indicates that she had made Jesus the source of strength that enabled her to maintain her busy life. Her ability to focus beyond the many things pulling at her to what was genuinely important enabled her to live with sweet assurance and precious calmness in spite of the whirlwind around her.

If we are to be Christlike, to have an influence with others, then our relationship with Him must take precedence over every other activity, no matter how important other activities seem or how loudly they may cry for our attention. When we study the outstanding and influential women of the Bible, we see that prayer seems to be the most common attribute—the ability to truly focus on Christ not only for our needs but also to express our worship and adoration of Him. How can we as women who desire to be influential be like these great women? By choosing to make progress in the daily, private practice of prayer. More than merely calling on God in times of crises, prayer must become a consuming passion in our lives.

Pardon My Progress

Have you ever noticed this little sign while shopping? Businesses often post a sign to let us know what's going on: Pardon Our Progress! After a few days or weeks, shopping in that store is easier and perhaps more enjoyable. Similarly, prayer helps me make progress in my spiritual intimacy with God. So that's what we must do; post a sign! Even if you don't hang the inscription on your front door, it si needs to be etched upon your heart.

Nothing is more important in the life of the Christi than regularly engaging in the privilege of prayer. Not just meaningless repetition, but consistent contact with, communion with, and fellowship with God.

Personally, I have found that I have no effectiveness in my public ministry without daily private prayer time. To try to influence others without first being fueled by the power of God through prayer is like trying to pour fresh water from an empty pitcher.

Oswald Chambers, in his classic *My Utmost for His Highest* puts it this way—"My worth to God in public is what I am in private."

Are you ready to make that choice? To progress further onward, my encouragement to you is: No matter what your day holds—make an appointment with God somewhere within your daily schedule. Be very specific; don't try to just "fit it in." Schedule your time with God as you would anyone else in your calendar, planner, or PDA. Write it in the first space on your To Do list. With all the new and helpful ways to schedule our time, there should be no excuses. I use this principle to my advantage by visually seeing when I've penciled in my time with Christ.

International speaker and author Becky Tirabassi has shared for years what prayer and its phenomenal results have done for her life. She drastically changed her schedule to include daily one-hour appointments with God—rather than haphazardly calling upon Him at times when she *rely*

ɔm her book, *Let Prayer Change Your Life*,
...agraph describes how Becky feels about her
...ities:

...tle did I know what I was asking for when I made
...imple decision to pray for an hour each day. ... as
my priorities realigned themselves, my vision cleared
and I could see forever! Time with God proved invaluable in the area of dreaming big dreams and believing
that with God's help they were possible, even though a
shadow of the past tended to shade any self-confidence
and adventuresome spirit that dared to dream.

In fact, now that I have seventeen years to look
back upon, I have come to the conclusion that the
very day I made the non-negotiable decision to have
a one-hour appointment with the living God was the
day I stepped onto the path of fulfilling the deepest
desires of my heart.

As my renewed priorities fell into place, my life's
purpose gained shape. I could see, pray for, and take
daily steps toward achieving what I hoped for and
what I could not see but looked forward to with complete assurance and inner conviction. I changed from
failing to plan and not see any results to being an
organized planner of my time and accomplishing
goals.[7]

Adjusting your life to the priority of prayer instead of
other human desires will not diminish what you get accomplished in your day. To the contrary, you will find yourself

able to get much more done. With a greater, more focused perspective from journaling and praying, you are able to show much more progress at the end of your God-given twenty-four hours. Letting go of nonessentials helps us all focus on life with eyes of eternity rather than urgency.

Why not begin your days with a prayer such as this:

"Lord, *how* is it that You want me to be a GIFT to today? Father, I fully realize that I don't have what it takes to be a gift to anyone without your help. Only You can make me the woman I long to be. Fill me with Your love so that out of my heart might flow gifts of love, joy, kindness, patience, goodness, faithfulness, gentleness, and self-control."

CONNECTING THE DOTS OF PRAYER

Those who know me personally ask, "So how does this sanguine personality, who dislikes sitting still and really likes to have fun, find the discipline and quiet time to pray?" You may be struggling with the same perseverance. It's not easy for any woman in the twenty-first century. But it also may not be as hard as you might think. So let's simplify the complex question of prayer with answers from the Lord himself.

Where Shall I Pray?

At first it sounds like a simple question with an even simpler answer—pray anywhere! But if it is that simple, why don't we do it? As you study the life of Jesus, you find a man who had every reason in the world to not have time to pray, yet He always made time for what was important. Luke 5:16

tells us, "But Jesus often withdrew to lonely places and prayed." Isn't it amazing that Jesus, as thronged by the crowds as He often was, still found a way to escape to pray alone. We are busy too. But we must be creative about finding places to pray. I love sitting on my pink floral couch in my little parlor with Bible and journal in hand, or on the deck watching the serenity of the near-by lake, or down on my knees beside my bed. But those places are not always possible, for me or for you.

Some days my solitary place becomes my car en route to the airport or running errands on the other side of our city. My car turns into one of the most sacred sanctuaries where I listen to uplifting praise music. No one can reach me and Jesus and I have wonderful conversations. I am able to talk to Him about my husband, decisions, and fears.

If you're a mom of young children, why not use the common activity of changing diapers as a call to prayer. Babies and toddlers love to hear the sound of their mother's voice. Think of how many prayers could be going up to God for the next generation of leaders if every young mom would use each diaper change as a prompting to pray for her young child? As a newly expectant first-time grandmother, I'm committing to do just that when our new little pink or blue bundle arrives! I can hardly wait (Rob says that's putting it mildly)!

"But, Sharon," as a young mom told me recently, "I have three children under the age of six and there's no block of time in my day to lock myself in a room to pray." Being "alone" can be a state of mind, it does not have to be a location. Become creative at finding your place of solitude. A short list of Bible characters demonstrates to us that one can pray just about anywhere! Jonah prayed in a fish; Daniel prayed in a lions' den; David prayed in a cave; Shadrach, Meshach, and Abednego prayed in a furnace! Paul prayed in the middle of a road; Jesus prayed in a garden; and John prayed on a deserted island. The simple point is this—you can pray anywhere. While your mind will try to make excuses, your heart must lead you to do it—anywhere!

How Shall I Pray?

But must I kneel? Do I fold my hands? Do I use archaic language? How do I pray? One of the clearest verses of Scripture on the subject is beautifully given to us in Matthew 6:5. Eugene Peterson has beautifully rendered the passage this way: "And when you come before God, don't turn that into a theatrical production either. All these people making a regular show out of their prayers, hoping for stardom! Do you think God sits in a box seat?" (MSG).

What a striking and convicting paraphrase. We're not to make a drama production out of prayer, nor are we to pray for show. Jesus paints a word picture of how we are to pray in the story of the tax collector and the Pharisee given in Luke 18. While the Pharisee stood with his proud manner, "strutting his stuff" before the Creator of the world, we are told the tax collector "would not even look up to heaven." The point is this: we are to pray with no confidence in ourselves. All of our confidence must be in the merit of the Lord Jesus Christ. If we come to God like the proud Pharisee, who thought he was worthy, God will not hear us! We are to come to God in humble surrender of ourselves and earnestly pray as needy people.

While the Pharisee was proudly proclaiming his value to God, the tax collector simply and humbly approached God, admitting his sin and failure. Instead of hiding his sin and boasting of his accomplishments, he acknowledged his shortcomings and in doing so found favor, forgiveness, and a listening ear with God. By recognizing his insignificance apart from Christ, he gained an audience with the king!

Don't misunderstand or go to an extreme with this passage of Scripture. We are not told here that we have no value. Each of us has been created in God's image, and as such each is wonderfully made. As women and moms and daughters and workers we have great opportunity to have an incredible impact in our places of influence. But sin has marred the beautiful creation God made. Because of His great love for us, because we represented great worth to the Savior, he remade His beautiful creation by going to the cross for us. Imagine, the Creator, the king of the universe, considered me of such exquisite value that He sacrificed His Son on Calvary so that my sins could be forgiven and I could reach my fullest potential. Now that's incredible! He gives us incredible worth, and adds value to what was valueless without Him.

We should also pray with clean hearts. If we aren't careful we can allow the closets of our heart to become as cluttered as the ones in our homes. This "spiritual clutter" can really hinder our ability to connect with Christ. King David rightly said, "If I had cherished sin in my heart, the Lord would not have listened" (Ps. 66:18). Sin, whether great and public or small and seemingly insignificant, will block the intimacy that we need and desire so deeply. The reason is simple: knowing what we have hidden in the corner of our hearts, we will keep those parts of our life secret from Him. Of course, this is silly, because He already knows our hearts—every inch, every corner, every hidden spot and stain—and loves us still! So be honest with Him, and He will welcome you with open arms. The heart needs to be cleansed before we bring our petitions to Him. In the New Testament, the apostle Peter considered this same thought when he quoted Psalm 34, "For the eyes of the Lord are on the righteous and his ears are attentive to their prayer, but the face of the Lord is against those who do evil" (1 Peter 3:12).

We are also warned in Scripture that God turns His eyes and His ears from those who refuse to confess sin. "Surely the arm of the LORD is not too short to save, nor his ear too dull to hear. But your iniquities have separated you from your God" (Isa. 59:1–2).

When Shall I Pray?

The answer is obvious! We are to pray—any time, anywhere, whether to acknowledge a wrongdoing, to petition for a need that presents itself, or to praise the One we serve. The psalms provide many timely examples of when we should pray. One of these examples is found in Psalm 91:

> I will say of the Lord, "He is my refuge and my
> fortress, my God, in whom I trust.
>
> Surely he will save you from the fowler's snare
> and from the deadly pestilence.
>
> He will cover you with his feathers,

and under his wings you will find refuge;
his faithfulness will be your shield and
rampart.

You will not fear the terror of night,
nor the arrow that flies by day,
nor the pestilence that stalks in the
darkness, nor the plague that destroys
at midday.

Incredible! Seven times we are told in this precious chapter what *God will do* for us if we will just set our love upon Him and call on Him. Don't you find that refreshing? Like David, we have struggles in this life that can be overwhelming. How satisfying to know that God is available seven days a week, twenty-four hours a day. Sadly, how often have you felt all alone when facing your difficult moments? Yet, how wonderful to know that the woman who partners with Christ is never alone again—He never expects us to face *anything* alone again, nor will He ever desert us! We can call upon Him for help 24/7—anytime, anywhere. Our faithful commitment to Him in prayer is the most precious of privileges indeed.

A TRULY POWERFUL PARTNER

Women love relationships, don't we? Think about the fact that Jesus desires to have an intimate relationship with you. Times of prayer make this truly powerful relationship possible. Partnering with Him in private prayer gives you power to have a positive influence. In prayer, your spirit gains the courage to go through the door God may be opening for you. Prayer is never about having our own way, but about saying to God, "whatever your will is for me today—I want it. Lead me in *Your* way."

Satan truly fears that kind of prayer, and will do anything to hinder it! He knows that if he can keep you focused on your own plans, he has cut off your communication, intimacy, and power from God. So our enemy works tirelessly to engineer circumstances to keep you from your knees. He will cause all sorts of urgent and important interruptions and bring well-meaning activities to stand in your way. But remember, as we neglect prayer we will lose power. Satan, then, becomes the winner.

Can you relate to this prayer written by a fellow author-friend of mine? "Dear Lord, so far today I am doing pretty well. I haven't screamed at the kids or thrown anything in a burst of anger. I have not grumbled or gossiped or whined. I haven't been greedy or self-centered. I have not yet charged anything to the credit card, and I haven't pigged out on the chocolate cake in the refrigerator. However, in a few minutes I will be getting out of bed, and I am going to need your help to make it through the rest of the day. Amen."

God cares deeply about our every need and the desires of our heart. When we come with our appeals before Him in a spirit of faith and submission, we will have our every need met—that is His promise. Remember, He is an intimate, loving God—a true partner who has awesome plans for your life. His plans are full of hope, potential, and promise! You may not see incredible opportunities laid out for you right now, but you will as you continue bringing your petitions before Him.

Pray the Write Way

If you are like me, you find yourself easily distracted from praying. What helps me, and what I want to encourage you to do, is to write out your prayers in a journal. Have you noticed how often individuals in the Bible prayed out loud to God? While many believers speak to God in the silence of their minds, I have found that I can focus better if I whisper my prayer out loud. And for several years now I have written out my prayers in a journal. Writing out my daily love, affirmation, and tender intimate fellowship with God has added a refreshing joy to our relationship. By doing so you will find yourself better able to say on track and not be so easily distracted. You will also be surprised as you slow down and focus your thinking on what you want to say to God. If you are a visual learner, as I am, this can transform your prayer life!

By journaling your prayer to your God, you will find daily direction in your day by discussing plans and dreams with Him on paper and verbally. You will learn to love God with a love that will change you from the inside out. By letting Him love you through His Word and talking to Him verbally, you will better be able to handle the unexpected surprises in your day because your day has been laid out before Him.

It is critical to have the right journal format for you! Not just some formula that has worked for someone else. Whether on your computer software program, in a notebook, or on pieces of scratch paper in scribbled secret codes, find what works for you.

PRAYER IN A FISHBOWL

Yes! I married a minister. For thirty-one years our family has lived in a glass house, observed by well-meaning but sometimes critical people within our congregations. We also have two daughters who, of course, are perfect. They are supposed to play the piano, sing, have perfect manners, and rise up every morning calling their mother "Blessed" even though she does serve Hamburger Helper a hundred different ways, right?

Not always. Nothing teaches a mother how to pray quite like a prodigal child. Later in her teens, our Mindy became enamored with the glitter of values far different from the ones taught in our home and strayed into the dark and seamy side of life. Trying to explain what happened in her own words, she would say today that she had an "out-of-body experience." Without going into detail, it was horribly painful to watch our daughter inflict such deep, inexpressible pain upon herself and her family. And living in the "fishbowl" parsonage did not help. I learned many things about prayer during those eighteen months. During this time I learned the true meaning of losing control and surrendering my daughter to God (she was truly His daughter anyway!). As I prayed, the Lord focused my mind not on Mindy's sin, but on areas of my life that needed cleansing, and it was revolutionary for me. As we began to see small steps of repentance that later turned into a jog and then a full-fledged sprint to God, I saw the true power of God to turn any life around, and the true meaning of forgiveness—all through the power of prayer. Through prayer I experienced firsthand what I had taught so many times before—that if I would come to the Lord He would wrap me in His everlasting loving arms and provide a shelter to this weary mom. During this darkest of times, the Lord changed my habits of prayer.

Your problems may be different from mine. We are all at different places in our spiritual journeys, and every woman experiences different circumstances. But as we are in different stages in our spiritual walk our struggles affect us similarly. The death of a loved one may feel like a raging hurricane to a new believer and a simple shower to a seasoned saint who has already personally experienced God's faithfulness. In nature, a heavy rain shower may be a blessing for a bear in the forest but life-threatening to the fragile songbird. To an elderly woman the loss of a loved one can be handled with the grace of experience and maturity, but to a teen losing her first boyfriend it may feel like a tragedy has ended life itself! The point is this: though the causes of our pain may be different, the pain still hurts deeply, and we must demonstrate our dependence upon our heavenly Father to comfort and strengthen us through our intimate times of prayer and Bible study with Him.

RUN TO GOD, NOT FROM GOD

Even on our best "put together" day, our own talents and abilities are not enough for us to make an eternal influence in the lives of those we love. We desperately need to pray. God longs to accomplish "infinitely more than we would ever dare to ask or hope" (Eph. 3:20 NLT).

Because God loves you, He is for you. He does not belittle

you to prove that He is in charge. Even when you ignore him for an extended period, He does not shy away from you. He does not send down His wrath on every little mistake you make, and He is extremely patient. God will take each circumstance in your life and use it in a constructive way for your growth—not your defeat. And He will rejoice when you experience His power and strength.

Our enemy, Satan, will try to make you believe you are totally unworthy as a woman. He will try to rob you of the charm and dignity that makes you valuable to God. He will try to place fear and rejection in your mind, leading you to believe you are a nobody. Because of His influence, many women feel useless, insignificant, helpless, sinful, and discouraged.

But God *never* says, "Forget it! There's no hope for her." Rather, He joyously and patiently works with you and disciplines you in such a way that lets you know you can run to Him, and not farther away. And yes, He might even use an egg carton to remind you that He waits patiently for you to come running back to Him, no matter how long it takes.

THE SECRET OF A DAILY PERSONAL ENCOUNTER

Prayer and time in God's Word are the ladles we use to dip down into the deep well of refreshing spring water that will quench thirsty hearts. As women of God, we simply cannot pray and remain the same. We have no options when it comes to whether we should pray or not; our heavenly Father commands us to pray. More than a refuge in crisis, prayer should be as much a part of our daily routine as combing hair and putting on our lipstick. While our make-up beautifies and enhances the exterior, prayer cleanses and beautifies the inner spirit and nature and makes us pleasing to our family and others. It is wonderful to know that we can pray from any location in any position because God is ready to answer, strengthen, and provide comfort.

Have your favorite version of the Bible near you as you pray. You will find the Holy Spirit will lead you to precious places where God desires to speak to you through His Word. A two-way conversation takes place between you and God when Scripture and prayer are blended together. You will find great comfort in the psalms as you express your concerns to God in prayer. It is in the psalms that I find the words to reach out to my Father's hand when I'm insecure and afraid. Those passages in the psalms help me put into words exactly what I may not be able to express otherwise.

In God's Word you will find guidance and answers to questions you bring before Him in prayer. Scripture further gives you the patience and perseverance you need while in God's waiting room, waiting in anticipation for God's answer or His timing. "In all your ways acknowledge him, and he will make your paths straight (Prov. 3:6).

I am not naive enough to assume that prayer is natural or easy for you. For whatever the reason—doubt, misunderstandings, fear from experiences in your past—prayer may be difficult for you. Perhaps you think God's Word applies to everyone except you. Or maybe your church experience or religious training was in a shame-based church. One beautiful woman in Canada shared with me that she "still remembered predominant verses quoted loudly and often by a very critical mother." This mistaken mom would use Scripture out of context to scold her daughter and humiliate her. Such unkind and ungodly rage caused the shining truths of scripture to be eclipsed by hardness and difficulty. God's Word had been misused and misapplied in her life, and it caused this sweet lady to have a misguided understanding of her heavenly Father.

I recently met another woman in her fifties whose father had screamed Scripture at her in anger. This woman recalls her daddy forcefully thundering in her ear, "Children are to obey their parents!" even during physical and sexual abuse to her. This man misused Scripture as a whip to control and dishonored the Bible in his daughter's mind. It took years for her to understand and clear up the confusion when as an adult she was unable to search out the truth about God. She came away from her early religious training feeling suppressed, depressed, oppressed, and repressed.

I share this precious secret of prayer because the sincere longing of my heart is that more and more women and young girls will grow into womanhood hearing how precious they are, how loved they are, and how gifted they are, instead of hearing what's wrong with them and where they fall short. That's the gift precious intimacy in a relationship with God brings. Make a definite commitment this moment to spend time with Him. As you read His Word, study Him, understand Him, recognize Him, love Him. And as you speak to Him through prayer, let the intimate experience impact you. Then you will find yourself influencing others.

PRAISE

A GIFTed woman wraps herself in a pleasant
package of PRAISE.

*Purposely choose to develop an attitude of true thankfulness in
all circumstances of life.*

Leadership expert John Maxwell loves to tell the simple story of a grandpa and grandma who visited their
grandchildren. Each afternoon Grandpa would lie down
for a nap. One day, as a practical joke, the grandkids
decided to put Limburger cheese in his mustache. Quite
soon he awoke sniffing. "Why, this room stinks," he
exclaimed as he got up and went out into the kitchen. He
wasn't there long until he decided that the kitchen
smelled too, so he walked outdoors for a breath of fresh

air. Much to Grandpa's surprise, the open air brought no relief, and he proclaimed, "The whole world stinks!"

Influencers in life are people who have a positive contentment in their spirit. Every one of us has had negative circumstances in life and obstacles to overcome. But our success and, more importantly, our happiness in life, are not determined by the circumstances we face, but by our responses to those circumstances.

I spent so much of my early adulthood being a very negative, even depressed person. I spent way too much time feeling ungrateful and more like a victim than a victor in Christ Jesus. Over a period of time, and I am sure with the prayers of my family and others, I began to realize how my attitudes were seriously hurting myself and others. I sat down at my kitchen table one day to determine what I needed to do to change. I knew it had to begin with my chronic thankless attitude. "Lord, please help me to change. I can no longer stand the sound of my own ungratefulness. Help me! I've made life unnecessarily difficult for myself and my family by all this fretting and fuming."

I desperately wanted to change, but first, my internal thinking patterns needed to be altered. "If only" replayed over and over in my mind. "If only I had a better, bigger home." "If only I had finished college before marriage." "If only my life weren't so stressful and hectic." "If only I could control my kids and get my husband to help out more." "If only I didn't have this health problem." And what I was really saying all along—"If only life were perfect!"

It was always something. I lived life as if the world rested on my shoulders. Peace, contentment, thanksgiving—these were not words I liked to talk about very much. I'd always thought that if I tried hard enough and long enough, I could make everything all right and please everybody, and everybody would like me, and life would be grand! And I would try with every ounce of strength that I could muster. But in my mind I failed. Truthfully, because I struggled with my attitude about myself, I assumed that others didn't like me either.

Actually, at the deepest level of my soul was my need for constant approval, because I had a strong fear of being abandoned. I had always found something imperfect and negative about myself, so it was natural that I began doing the same—finding fault—in all my relationships. By the end of my twenties I was engulfed by what Zig Ziglar calls "stinkin' thinkin'"—detrimental, damaging thought patterns about myself and others. I was convinced that the glass was half empty and no one could convince me otherwise.

As I began to pray and seek advice from others, it became apparent that I had never been able to walk beyond a painful period of my childhood—the time after my birth mother died. My desire is to share these very personal thoughts with you in the hope that they may encourage you or someone you may influence.

Following my mother's death, my sister and I were housed at various people's homes in our church or at the homes of relatives for lengthy periods of time. Both my mother and father were the only children in their families, so these relatives were distant to us, and not ones we were used to being around. It was at this time in my life that I began to distrust anyone and everyone.

As a young child, I didn't question what was going on, nor did I understand what was happening. Outwardly, I just smiled and tried to please everyone. But it never seemed to be enough. All I knew was that no one seemed to want me to stay with them for long periods of time. In my mind, I felt bad. I was the reason my mother left me, and I was the reason no one wanted me around. I always felt like I was letting people down. Imagine the feelings of insecurity that emerged as I matured.

The roles reversed when I had two daughters of my own. Still trying to please, I overdosed on trying harder and harder to be a good mom. To keep them from ever thinking badly of me (because I still feared being abandoned), I would go to almost any extreme to avoid conflict with my daughters. Eventually, the fear and anger of my early life turned into clinical depression. It was years before I could openly admit when speaking before audiences that I experienced weeks of hospitalization and months of outpatient counseling that finally allowed God's healing in my life. Now I realize that this early emotional pain has dramatically impacted who I am, and has allowed me to minister to many dear women in similar circumstances. Undoubtedly, what Satan had hoped to use in my life to ruin me, God turned into a beautiful tapestry that is a trophy of His grace and purpose. I learned to make a conscious effort to surround myself with positive and uplifting friends, and to use Scripture to reprogram and replace my negative mind.

As you determine to cultivate a thankful heart, you will begin to notice that those who seem consistently happy have general qualities that set them apart from others:

1. They smile a lot.

2. They make others feel important when they are together.

3. They give sincere compliments and praise.

4. They are genuinely interested in others.

5. They have a thankful spirit, even when life isn't so good.

6. They say the words, "thank you" to others a lot.

7. They believe what God says about them, instead of people's opinions.

8. They know and believe God's Word.

The best cure for ungratefulness is to turn outward to others and stop dwelling on the inward ME so much. Have you ever developed an ingrown toenail? It hurts. Even the simplest activity becomes a rigorous chore because of the pain that seems to spread through your foot, up your leg and into your entire body! Isn't it amazing that such a small ingrown area of the body can cause so much pain? Turning inward emotionally over a long period of time can cause even greater damage. A toenail is comparatively easy to fix in contrast to the emotional pain of inward depression that can darken the very light of life in the deep shadows of one's mind.

SWITCH THE STATION

The happiest people I know say "thank you" often, so I began doing the same. Often. By doing so, I opened myself more to others. From the clerk in the department store to my husband and my daughters—the response was nothing short of amazing. Our home took on a fresh and beautiful aspect as, more and more, God changed me from within with this attitude of gratitude.

When you are watching a TV show with your children that gets too scary or violent, what do you do? You switch the station to a happier, more appropriate program. We can decide to do the same with our negative, pessimistic attitude. Why not switch the station of your mind from negativism to a positive praise channel?

We can combat negativism by making a conscious effort to root out our negative thoughts and replace them with principles and true joy and peace. God's Word, the Truth, will replace the old, worn-out lies that our minds begin to believe. It is then that we can live our lives with gratitude, full of praise for the One who is Truth.

Each time you dwell on past failures and errors or adverse circumstances in the present, your mind begins to think negatively. By an act of your will you can accept the challenge to turn your mind over to the positive things that God does for you and is currently doing in your life. By writing down His blessings in a journal on a regular basis, even if just one praise each day, you will become conscious of His many benefits given to you each day. Writing out "I'm thankful for …" is a great antidote for depression. I know from experience that this new perspective will change your life and the lives of those you influence.

During several weeks while hospitalized in despair and depression, I began to apply these principles personally and take small tiny steps to offer thanksgiving to God. A smile from a nurse, a phone call from a loved one, or even encouragement from one of the professional counselors all became little bits of praise that eventually became a flood of gratitude. Thanksgiving offered in private during my own quiet time with the Lord became a healing balm bringing melodious restoration to my soul. "Even in moments of crisis, a grateful attitude transforms you," says Sarah Breathnach in her book, *Simple Abundance, A Daybook of Comfort and Joy.*[8]

Have you ever noticed how different attitudes are during the Thanksgiving holiday season? We send cards and call to mind the many ways we are thankful to God for His blessings. It changes the way we see our world. Attitudes seem to improve, at least for one holiday week each year.

CONFESSIONS OF A NEG-A-HOLIC

When God wants to get our attention, things often get worse before they get better. Saying thanks at mealtimes has been a part of my lifestyle as long as I can remember. But it wasn't until a year ago as I write this, when Rob and I were between ministries, that I truly learned that a blessing before meals is not just a memorized prayer to feel spiritual. God put us in a position and time in our lives when we couldn't help but depend upon Him. Feeling deserted and alone, and with no substantial source of income, we found His place of true peace and joy. During that special yet very lean nine months, we were made keenly aware of divine provision for our family. God orchestrated our circumstances so that He was our only provider, and He came through for us!

Sometimes, we have to suffer great defeat to appreciate the little victories in life. Never forget that God is more interested in our character than our comfort. His goal is for us to get to know Him, our provider, and to become more and more like Him. God will use overwhelming sadness and difficult times to get our full attention. I am certainly no expert, but I've come to believe that God does what it takes in each of our lives for us to learn our sufficiency is in Him.

It pays to clean out your junk drawer once in a while. I found this little saying recently while reorganizing: "I had no shoes, and complained, until I met a man who had no feet." This forces us to keep things in perspective, doesn't it?

As Christians, we are mandated to make the choice to be thankful. First Thessalonians 5:18 (NASB) gives the command (not a suggestion) "in everything give thanks; for this is God's will for you in Christ Jesus." Many have asked, "How, Lord, can I be thankful when my world is falling apart?"

The Bible never teaches that we will be problem-free. In fact, Scripture seems to indicate that those who make a conscientious effort to live for Christ will endure many different kinds of trials. A commitment to a grateful and praising heart does not mean that we have to jump for joy when something negative happens. History has proven and the Bible virtually proves that bad things do happen to good people. But with Christ in our hearts we have the inner peace that sustains us and enables us to say, "I may not like this—I may not have chosen this, but God is in control. I can trust Him. And I can praise Him because He knows what He's doing."

Picture this scene in heaven: There is panic around the throne of God. The seraphim and cherubim are fluttering nervously in all directions; Michael, that great archangel, walks back and forth before the throne wringing his hands while Gabriel is shouting panicked instructions into the heavenly hotline. God the Father sits with a look of anger while His Son says with great consternation, "Oh no, what are we going to do?"

That's hard to picture because it won't happen! What a wonderful privilege to know that in all of history the hosts of heaven have never heard God say, "Oops!" His Word is filled with precious promises about His ability to direct the affairs of men and angels with a loving heart and steady hands. When you are able to live in light of those facts, you will realize that although the pain may be great at the time, there is One who is in constant control of our circumstances, and you can bring your trust and praises to Him. You can have a sense of peace that God is going to bring good out of every situation.

A PROMISE IS A PROMISE

May God remind us daily, no matter what obstacles we face, that we are empowered by the One who freely gives us all good and gracious gifts. All of us know people who seem to have a positive mental attitude no matter what the circumstances of life bring. Through hard times and tough situations, these people seem to hold on to hope by delighting in

God's Word. You will find one of the most striking examples of this in Mary, the mother of Jesus.

As a young teenage girl she faced a major interruption in her life—she was going to be a mother. Not just any mother, but the mother of the Messiah. Such an honor was unimaginable, but it must have come at a great price. Imagine trying to convince your parents, relatives, friends, and fiancé that your pregnancy was by the Holy Spirit! Remember, this was in a day when unwed pregnancies resulted in being expelled from society and often stoned to death! Mary's pregnancy would bring shame to her fiancé and her family for years to come. This was a serious issue.

And what proof could Mary present to her critics? Remember that Jesus did not begin his earthly ministry of miracles until He was thirty years old. Until that time He was no doubt a charming and extremely intelligent young man, but no one suspected He was the sinless Son of God, except perhaps Mary and Joseph.

Even after he began his earthly ministry and revealed Himself to be the Son of God through powerful signs and miracles, most did not believe Him. His rejection was cruel and harsh, and His ultimate death by crucifixion was considered a public disgrace. This poor young girl must have experienced years of ridicule and harassment. Yet you never find her complaining about her circumstances or asking for a way out. In a passage that has come to be known as Mary's Song, we learn incredible insight into her humble and grateful heart: "My soul glorifies the Lord and my spirit rejoices in God my Savior, for he has been mindful of the humble state of his servant. From now on all generations will call me blessed, for the Mighty One has done great things for me—holy is his name" (Luke 1:46–49).

That's it. No bitterness. No criticism. No embarrassment. Only simple gratitude and praise. Though it would have been impossible for her to understand all of the implications that this pregnancy would mean for her future, she showed incredible maturity and complete trust in God.

Perhaps the most striking characteristic about the great missionary spokesman, the apostle Paul, was his ability to remain content and thankful while enduring almost endless persecution at the hands of his enemies. Concerning these circumstances, he once wrote, "Since I know it is all for Christ's good, I am quite content with my weaknesses and with insults, hardships, persecutions, and calamities. For when I am weak, then I am strong" (2 Cor. 12:10 NLT).

Although one of the most educated men of his day, Paul never felt like God owed him anything. Paul's difficulties would have given many opportunities to conclude that God is not fair. But instead, Paul trusted Christ with every moment of his life, and in so doing gained respect and influence everywhere he went. After telling the believers in Philippi the reasons why he could have had confidence in his own abilities, he states: "I once thought all these things were so very important, but now I consider them worthless because of what Christ has done. Yes, everything else is worthless when compared with the priceless gain of knowing Christ Jesus my Lord. I have discarded everything else, counting it all as garbage, so that I may have Christ and become one with him" (Phil. 3:7–9 NLT).

You may be thinking, "Well that's just not me! I always tend to see the negative side of things and I just can't help myself." You may be surprised to learn that Paul was not always a positive individual either. In fact, he tells us that his contentment was a learned character quality. He writes, "for I have learned to be content whatever the circumstances" (Phil. 4:11).

Contentment is not a natural quality for most people. But you will find that as you turn your focus away from your bad experiences and focus on Christ, your entire being will begin to change. The inner beauty that God has always desired for you will quickly work its way through your spirit and begin to radiate through outward countenance and actions to others. The influence that you have always desired will suddenly materialize, and you will develop a magnetism that will bring others with you on your spiritual journey to Christlikeness. The transformation that you will experience will be nothing short of a miracle, and you will find satisfaction, contentment, and completeness in your relationships with Christ, your family, and your friendships.

JUMP-START YOUR JOY!

David did not always experience God's peace. We know from history and from the Bible that his character was not always what it should be. Like ours, his life was a roller-coaster ride of ups and downs, from victory to defeat to victory again. In spite of his often traumatic circumstances, many times brought about by his own disobedience, David

displays for us a beautiful example of gratitude as he journals his praise and thanksgiving. The psalms, many of which
David wrote, are filled with the language of prayer. Let the
following phrases from Scripture jump start your praise and
let them become yours to flow to your heavenly Father:

I will give you thanks in the great assembly;
among throngs of people I will praise you. (Ps. 35:18)

We give thanks to You, O God, we give thanks, for your
Name is near; men tell of your wonderful deeds. (Ps. 75:1)

Give thanks to the Lord, for he is good;
His love endures forever.
Give thanks to the God of gods.
His love endures forever.
Give thanks to the Lord of lords:
His love endures forever.
(Ps. 136:1–3)

Let us come before him with thanksgiving and extol him
with music and song.
(Ps. 95:2)

Enter his gates with thanksgiving and his courts with praise;
give thanks to him and praise his name.
(Ps. 100:4)

THE MISERY OF INGRATITUDE

Throughout his earthly ministry Jesus did miracles for
others. He healed, he delivered from Satanic oppression, he
provided for needs. Countless lives were changed because
Jesus saw and met needs. Out of the many whom Jesus

healed, only a few actually expressed gratitude. Once such occasion is found in Luke's gospel. In Jesus' day leprosy was considered a terrible social disease, perhaps even worse than the terrible AIDS virus of today. Because it was such an infectious disease, people with leprosy were restricted in their activity and pronounced unclean. They had to walk on the other side of the road when approached by someone from another direction, and had to announce to anyone coming in their direction that they were "unclean." You can imagine the social consequences that such a disease would bring upon their livelihood. Victims of leprosy often lived as beggars, sleeping in shanty communes outside the cities near the garbage at night, and begging at the corners of busy streets during the day. So it would make sense that one delivered from such a terrible plight would demonstrate his joy and thankfulness wildly. But that wasn't always the case. Let's pick up our story in Luke 17:11-19:

> Now on his way to Jerusalem, Jesus traveled along the border between Samaria and Galilee. As he was going into a village, ten men who had leprosy met him. They stood at a distance and called out in a loud voice, "Jesus, Master, have pity on us!"
>
> When he saw them, he said, "Go, show yourselves to the priests." And as they went, they were cleansed.
>
> One of them, when he saw he was healed, came back, praising God in a loud voice. He threw himself at Jesus' feet and thanked him—and he was a Samaritan.
>
> Jesus asked, "Were not all ten cleansed? Where are

the other nine? Was no one found to return and give praise to God except this foreigner?" Then he said to him, "Rise and go; your faith has made you well."

Did you catch it? Only one in ten said "thank you" to Christ for healing them of their disease. It is a picture of ingratitude at its worst. By failing to recognize the source of their blessing the nine ungrateful lepers missed out on the incredible joy and blessing of fellowship with the great Healer. How often have we failed to recognize God's activity in our life? How often have you been delivered from desperate events and negative experiences only to go along your merry way with no thought about the One who brought precious deliverance into your life?

A CHOICE EVERY DAY

Years ago doctors Frank Minirth and Paul Meier brought us their best-selling book, *Happiness Is a Choice*.[9] In it they challenged every one of us to do just that—make a choice. There are times when our choosing must come out of a grief-stricken heart. At other times we are called on to be thankful in spite of a troubled mind. And at other times it may be though enduring a pain-filled, suffering body. But, underlying all human tragedy for the believer is the loving heavenly Father's grace-filled plan for our lives.

In these tough times we find praying Scripture is the only way we can begin to thank God for His unlimited goodness. We need the exhortation of 2 Thessalonians 2:13 in our prayers. "But we ought always to thank God for you, brothers loved by the Lord, because from the beginning God chose you to be saved through the sanctifying work of the Spirit and through belief in the truth." And let's not forget to include, "always giving thanks to God the Father for everything, in the name of our Lord Jesus Christ" (Eph. 5:20).

The apostle Paul further suggests that the spirit of thanksgiving is to accompany all we do as a testimony for Christ and as an offering to the Lord. He issues a challenge to every one of us: "And whatever you do, whether in word or deed, do it all in the name of the Lord Jesus, giving thanks to God the Father through him" (Col. 3:17).

"Too many people are too busy worrying about the rain coming tomorrow to enjoy the sunshine today." That quote from an unknown source characterizes how many women struggle with a thankful spirit. I want to challenge you to allow your heart to be filled with a godly gratitude more than just on Thanksgiving Day. Begin keeping a list for yourself. This day is the best day to begin. Get yourself a brand new journal and title the first page, "Today I Am Thankful For ..." Begin to write down little blessings, tiny steps in a positive direction. Each day for one week write down your expressions of gratefulness—at least three items each day. You will soon find yourself noticing human kindnesses and God's goodness in your life in ways you never noticed before. You'll be shocked at what a difference it will make within your thought life—and outside on your face. Helen Keller, blind and deaf, once said, "Keep your face to the sunshine and you cannot see the shadow." With God's help will you determine right now to "keep your face to the sunshine?" The results will be revolutionary!

As I was writing this chapter, Rob and I took a break and visited an antique store. As we were leaving the store, a sign on the door caught my attention: "If You Are Grouchy, Irritable, Or Just Plain Mean There Will Be A $10 Fee For Putting Up With You."

I loved that sign! It made us laugh, but it also made us think. I wanted to take it home to remind us of its message. I'm afraid that if my family and friends were honest, they would report times when they should have charged me $10 for being so grouchy! Perhaps they deserved it for having to put up with me.

In these many times of difficulty, seeing anything to be thankful for was often eclipsed by my asking, "Why me, Lord?" I'm now learning to see God's hand at work in the midst of all the year's uncertainty and turmoil. Nothing robs us from being truly thankful more than asking "why?" I'm learning to accept that if God doesn't tell me the reasons why, then I must not need to know. He has promised to "meet all your needs according to his glorious riches in Christ Jesus" (Phil. 4:19), hasn't He? When will I learn that He knows what I need even better than I do?

It's one thing to offer thanks because it's the right thing to do, and it's another to be sincerely thankful. That's what I'm trying to learn—to be truly thankful and full of praise even when it's not easy. In the middle of recent trials I have found it harder than ever before to be thankful. At the close of some days, my simple prayer was, *Lord, thank you that I made it through this day!* There have been many days when I had to ask Him for an attitude adjustment. It meant praying for a thankful spirit toward the people and events that meant me harm and had caused intense pain. I am a bit embarrassed to admit such ingratitude when I owe Christ such a debt for all He's done for me.

These are lessons I seem to learn over and over in my life. When my faith is weak and especially, those times when my body is physically weak, choosing to have a thankful, praising spirit gives profound comfort through the nearness of the Holy Spirit. If I will give up my aching heart to Him, He is able to transform it. My goal is to keep doing that for my husband, my family, my friends, because you can't give away a gift to others that you don't already have yourself.

PATIENCE

A GIFTed woman is continually learning PATIENCE—
waiting on God's timing; trusting that in time,
God will make clear His glorious plan.

"I need patience and I want it right now!"

I have to snicker at the familiarity of those words. We've all said them, probably more often than we'd like to admit. But after my snickering comes a long, silent sigh. I have always disliked waiting. In God's waiting room I hear God speak clearly to my heart, saying firmly, "Sharon, you are very anxious." I counter back, "I have reason to be!" Then I proceed to cry out the helplessness that I feel in just marking time. Though my impatient nature abhors waiting, how comforting it is to know that when God puts me on hold, His patience with me is incredible. He reminds me over and over, whispering, "Trust Me. My way is not always what you have on your agenda."

No doubt you've had experiences where God's plan seemed obscured—days upon days going about the tasks before you while waiting for something to happen. Then nothing happens. That's when the words, "Don't just sit there. Do something—and do it now!" seem to ring in our heads, distracting us from learning what God has for us in a waiting period. The result of patience is *always* something good for us in the long term.

I'm finding that there is only one way to learn patience. The hard way. It takes a lifetime of trial and error because our ability to see ahead is often clouded by our own irresponsibility and selfishness. God often uses painfully slow, day-to-day experiences to shape, mold, and develop the Christian character trait of patience in us. Recently my devotional times have reminded me to *let God be at work within my life. Be patient, God is not finished with you yet.* (Some of you will remember pins we used to wear some twenty-five years ago at seminars with that slogan on them.) Seems as though all the Scriptures and auxiliary reading I've been doing in my quiet time lately has set my heart smack-dab in the front row in the classroom marked "PATIENCE 101."

Okay, it's true confession time. I really need patience. I'm as guilty as the next woman. Maybe that's why this classroom called Patience 101 is completely full. Look around; there's not one empty seat in the room. Are you one who races frantically through life impatient with any dillydallying of others because, after all, you're terribly busy? After all, you've got things to do and places to go and people to see.

Me, too.

I demand, "Now!" God answers, "Wait." I cry "Do something!" God replies, "Stay still." I scream, "Gimmee!" God says, "Be content." That's when I feel immobilized in a fog of indecision and confusion. *And I don't like it.*

I waste a lot of energy frantically trying to cross off items on my To-Do list. I'm impatient with anyone and anything that gets in the way of my being able to conform the world to *my* agenda. I rather enjoy punching a button to open my car, then drive away, drive through, and drive on! Maybe you know just what I'm talking about. Heaven help the person who gets in the way of our to-do lists.

Waiting is never fun. These are the days of instant everything—from potatoes to rice to cereal to coffee. Unfortunately our instant society is producing some serious problems. Hurry-scurry attitudes trickle down to our spirituality to the point that many think they can achieve instant maturity. Ah, but this is one area that cannot be hurried. Just as a farmer knows not to expect instant reaping after he sows his seed, we must take whatever time is necessary to prepare, plant properly, and then patiently wait for God to do His work.

Billy Graham comments on the lack of patience that characterizes our generation:

> Patience is the ability to absorb strain and stress without complaint and to be left undisturbed by obstacles, delays, or failures. This is a high-strung, neurotic, impatient age. We hurry when there is no reason to

hurry—just to be hurrying. This fast-paced age has produced more problems and less morality than previous generations, and it has given us jangled nerves. Impatience has produced a crop of broken homes, ulcers, and has set the stage for more world wars.[10]

Even in an instant society, some things still take time. What are the areas God is using to grow your patience right now? Is your heart longing for, waiting for: a child, a new job, a husband, health, a home of your own, friends, financial security, physical beauty?

All of these things are good, but they are good only in God's timing. We need to adapt more and more to Christ's choices for our lives rather than our own. God often allows annoyances, difficulties, even suffering and trials, to come our way for a specific purpose. That purpose is to get our attention and help us develop a Christlike attitude for our growth in patience. As the Christian sees these trying times working to his advantage in achieving character virtues, the stage is set for the development of a patient spirit. For that, we can be thankful; yes, even celebrate! The very fact that our Creator loves us so deeply as to pursue our patience and Christlike character is beyond my imagination. "Consider it pure joy, my brothers, whenever you face trials of many kinds, because you know that the testing of your faith develops perseverance. Perseverance must finish its work so that you may be mature and complete, not lacking anything" (James 1:2–4).

You see, God is concerned about the bigger picture of our lives, not just the here and now, and He is committed to seeing us develop the following Christlike virtues in our lives:

CHRISTLIKE VIRTUES—JAMES 3:17

Virtue	Opposite
pure	impure
peaceloving	impatient
considerate	harsh, unkind
submissive	unapproachable
full of mercy	unloving
good fruit	fruitless
impartial	wavering
sincere	dishonest

CHRISTLIKE VIRTUES—GALATIANS 5:22–23

Virtue	Opposite
love	hate
joy	unhappy spirit
peace	argumentative
patience	impatience
kindness	hardness
goodness	bad
faithfulness	legalism
gentleness	arrogance
self-control	undisciplined

Looking at the right column above makes me chime in with Paul when he said, "What a wretched man I am! Who will rescue me from this body of death?" I take a long, deep breath just knowing he answers his rhetorical question by exclaiming, "Thanks be to God—through Jesus Christ our Lord." (Rom. 7:24–25). I can then claim His victory, His love, and His patience.

Being genuine followers of Jesus Christ means that we allow our spirits to be dominated by the Holy Spirit, not by self or the spirit of this world. Only then we might have grace to grow in each of the above virtues.

BEWARE OF QUICK FIXES

I look back now at all the times I could have been serving and trusting, but I selfishly disobeyed by getting ahead of God's plan. Not waiting and heeding God's timing, I gave up blessings and often missed out on what the voice of patience would have taught me. In one amazing passage of Scripture, God explains how to be content by resting in the arms of patience. This secret is found in Philippians 4:12–13:

"I know what it is to be in need, and I know what it is to have plenty. I have learned the secret of being content in any and every situation, whether well fed or hungry, whether living in plenty or in want" (v. 12).

Read on—lean in and let your eyes feast upon the most important part of this secret of patience. It is found in the next verse: "I can do everything through him who gives me strength" (v. 13).

God's strength—not mine. That's the secret—that's where patience comes in. Patience is the secret key that opens the door to contentment. When we rest in the arms of God for needed patience, He will give us strength.

Contentment follows right behind. When all throughout the day our minds are bombarded with distracting thoughts of discontent, patience comes forward and gives us the strength to wait for God's best. After years of waiting, watching, and working we find that God was there in our situation all the time. "Those who sow in tears will reap with songs of joy. He who goes out weeping, carrying seed to sow, will return with songs of joy, carrying sheaves with him" (Ps. 126:5-6).

Waiting is so much better than settling for what might seem humanly good *at the time.* Usually our quick fix is woefully contrary to God's perfect plan. Waiting means that God can get the glory, not we ourselves, after we've pushed and shoved and forced something into happening through human effort.

Sometimes God says yes when we pray. Sometimes he says no. Often he wants us to wait. While we are waiting we must remember that God is God and we are not. Did you get that? It bears repeating: God is God and we are not. One challenging speaker at a recent weekend retreat said it this way, "There is only one God, and it is not me!" We can accept God's timing best when we accept God as God and ourselves as human.

Take a look with me at people in the Scriptures who refused to wait and paid dearly:

- Esau missed the crown of his birthright;
- Moses missed going into the Promised Land;
- Saul lost his crown and the founding of a line
  of kings.

One of the most compelling illustrations of this lack of patience is found in Abraham's wife, Sarah. Now please don't misunderstand; she displayed incredible patience for many, many years to see God fulfill His promise of a son for Abraham. But as often happens with those of us who are frail and human, she finally had enough. She made a mess of things when she could not wait any longer for God to open her womb and give her a child. In trying to manipulate God's will, she offered Abraham her servant Hagar, and Hagar bore Abraham's child. But God's way prevailed. Despite Sarah's attempt at interference, God gave her the son he had promised.

While we're waiting, we can be rejoicing and praising, even when we are hemmed in with all kinds of troubles; these very troubles will develop patience in us. Discover what God has promised to give the patient: "... we also rejoice in our sufferings, because we know that suffering produces perseverance, perseverance, character; and character, hope" (Rom. 5:3–4).

PATIENCE BOTH IN TRAGEDY AND IN TRIUMPH

Pastor and author Scotty Smith says it best: "There is no growing in grace without groaning in grace." Rob and I were reminded once again several years ago as we saw a huge storm brewing all around us. We felt as though our ship was sinking. We prayed earnestly that God would stop the storm. He chose not to. We prayed that God would pick us up away from the storm and set us on dry ground. He chose not to do that either! I kicked, screamed, begged God. He did not budge us out of or remove our storm. Finally, I cried before God, "If this is something we must face, at least let me come out of it with more patience to face the days ahead."

That's when I began to learn this secret personally: With time, God's glorious plan becomes clearer. Trusting God when the storm rages is difficult but life-changing. After many months with the crashing waves beating all around us, Rob and I made it to shore. Our ship was battered, but God never let go of our hands or our hearts throughout the entire journey. During that time God gave me the opportunity to be as close to Him as I have ever been. Sometimes I would even visualize myself in the "hollow of His hand," as the old hymn says. In the unmet needs, expectations, and disappointments since, Jesus continues to remind me, "Sharon, be patient. In *My* time, this storm, too, will subside. I will keep you safe till the storm passes by."

By shifting our focus from what *we* do to what *God* is doing, patience can have its perfect work in our hearts. That's how my life can become a God-story, not a Sharon-story.

What makes you impatient? A bit of introspection and analysis on our part in regard to impatience may be revealing and helpful. Consider the following questions:

- **Am I** selfish, demanding, or expecting perfection from those I love? Remember: God is not finished with them yet either.

    > "Be patient with everyone. Make sure that nobody pays back wrong for wrong, but always try to be kind to each other and to everyone else" (1 Thess. 5:14–15).

- **Am I** easily irritated or irked because someone gets away with something?

> "Do not fret because of evil
> men or be envious of those who
> do wrong" (Ps. 37:1).

- **Am I** immature or petty about the little things in life?

> "But solid food is for the
> mature, who by constant use have
> trained themselves to distinguish
> good from evil" (Heb. 5:14).

- **Am I** jealous or envious of others?

> "Be patient and stand firm ...
> Don't grumble against each other,
> brothers, or you will be judged"
> (James 5:8–9).

- **Am I** dominated by the things of this world (materialism), impatient, and not content?

> "Since, then, you have been
> raised with Christ, set your hearts
> on things above, where Christ is
> seated at the right hand of God"
> (Col. 3:1).

- **Am I** angry when my self-sufficiency is threatened?

> "Blessed are the meek, for they
> will inherit the earth" (Matt. 5:5).

- **Am I** a person who has to have things or situations the way I want them, when I want them, rather than waiting on God's timing?

"Now we see but a poor reflection as in a mirror; then we shall
see face to face. Now I know in
part; then I shall know fully, even
as I am fully known" (1 Cor.
13:12).

Sitting in the Waiting Room

God's gifts to us are endless. Believing God's love to be
sovereign over every situation in our lives helps us to cultivate, nurture, and sustain a patient heart. It is often in the
very experience of extreme anxiety and adversity that we
must wait patiently upon the Lord. He often chips away at
our masterful methods of control. Let me introduce you to
a few of my friends who have humbly learned some hard lessons of patience even while they don't understand, when
they didn't see, or if things did not make sense to them.

Kathy and John: "Having a child was not how God could use us best."

Why does God permit his loved ones to suffer pain, such
as the pain of being unable to bear a child for over thirty
years of marriage? Kathy and John, dear friends of Rob's and
mine, will find out only when they get to heaven. Until then,
they do not stop trusting that the God of heaven is the same
God who lives in their hearts. Every Mother's Day Kathy
receives loving cards from those whom she's nurtured down
through the years. Life didn't go like she wanted, but Kathy
continues to encourage, pray with, and bear the pain of
other women who are unable to bear a child and want one

so badly. She understands. She is lovingly content. She's one of the most patient women I know. Kathy has learned patience through not having what she desperately desired, but knowing she didn't have to figure it all out for herself.

Maggie: "Taking my hands off of my husband means placing him in God's hands."

Why does God allow a Christian wife to wrap herself in a blanket on the couch, then pray for her unbelieving husband for more than an hour each morning for seventeen years? Maggie's never-ending faith is ever-deepening. She nurtures this faith by time, prayer, and God's Word. Some mornings she awakens at three or four in the morning and is unable to go back to sleep. She believes God arouses her for a special reason: to persevere in prayer. Those mornings this dear wife holds prayer meetings on her couch for many hours. Her husband notices; he doesn't even mind. And Maggie waits expectantly for her husband's salvation, which she believes by faith will come soon. At this writing she still prays patiently daily, then lets God be God.

Carol: "I decided to give up my right to be married."

Happily ever after? That's what Carol thought when she graduated from college, got her Master's degree, and landed a wonderful teaching job in a Bible college. But bit by bit, her perfect life began to crumble. There would be no more charades. She realized one piece to her perfect puzzle was missing. At an age and place in life when most women her age were happily married with a family of their own, she was still single and lonely. In her desperation, she tried to fill in the gaps with one man after another, but every relationship left her empty. Her heart longed for a man and she began to fill the void with everything this world has to offer.

Consumed with loneliness, Carol fell on her face before God feeling battle-scarred like the apostle Paul when he said, "... no one came to my support, but everyone deserted me" (2 Tim. 4:16). She now says, "God has kept me single as a gift to do a very special work for Him. I have learned that God is with me always, even unto the end of the world. I am not alone." Carol walks step by step, day by day, trusting God for the opportunity to travel with the college music teams every weekend; something she may not be able to do if her situation changes. She could question God and get angry, but she does not. Now her heart's cry is not "Give me a man," but "God, give me more of You."

Debbie and John: "I kept hoping and didn't ever want to give up!"

John was a high profile attorney in a large southern city, with an office overlooking the bay and all the other perks that go with such a lofty position. His wife, Debbie, was a successful and contented homemaker with three beautiful daughters. During a particularly busy time in John's life, Debbie and the girls became active in church and gave their hearts to Christ. When John heard of their faith he proceeded to ridicule and make fun of their newfound relationship. After repeated attempts to get John to visit their church or talk with their pastor, they patiently retreated and began to pray. And pray they did. For over ten years, Debbie was faithful to visit the altar at their church to pray for her husband. Through great difficulty she remained faithful to him even though there was no spiritual unity whatsoever.

Debbie was so faithful to visit the altar that even her own daughters were embarrassed by her repeated public display of concern for her husband. Unbelievably, one Sunday John showed up at church. After ten years of patient waiting and praying for the man she loved, Debbie walked forward with John in their church as he made a public profession of his newfound faith in Christ. Patience, perseverance, and prayer from a wife paid off in the saving faith of her husband. She commented that she felt like a newlywed all over again.

In her book, *Help, Lord, My Whole Life Hurts*, Carol Mayhall writes,

> Sometimes, in the fog of waiting, the lesson He will pound home to us is simply, *Do not be anxious*. Our own helplessness causes us to cry to Him to give us the strength and trust not to be anxious when everything within us screams with concern and apprehensiveness. Over and over He whispers, "Trust Me." It takes all our will—and great help from Him—to do just that.[11]

My soul shouts with Isaiah when he penned, "But those who hope in the Lord will renew their strength. They will soar on wings like eagles; they will run and not grow weary, they will walk and not be faint" (Isa. 40:31).

With the psalmist I exclaim:

> I waited patiently for the LORD;
>> he turned to me and heard my cry.
> He lifted me out of the slimy pit,
>> out of the mud and mire;

> he set my feet on a rock
> > and gave me a firm place to stand.
> He put a new song in my mouth,
> > a hymn of praise to our God.
> Many will see and fear
> > and put their trust in the LORD.
> > > (Ps. 40:1–3)

And with Peter I am thankful that "The Lord is not slow in keeping his promise, as some understand slowness. He is patient with you, not wanting anyone to perish, but everyone to come to repentance" (2 Peter 3:9).

THE UNLIMITED PATIENCE OF JESUS

Jesus shows us mercy each day—the same, patient mercy He displayed to us when "While we were still sinners, Christ died for us" (Rom. 5:8). We dare not forget that. God does not wait for us to become acceptable before He saves us. We would all still be lost. In perfect patience, not by force or selfish demands, He waits for us to call upon His name to claim Jesus as the Son of God. How liberating it would be in our relationships if we would do the same. Janette Oke, novelist, put it simply when she said, "Patience keeps us from running ahead of God."

The apostle Paul said it this way: "For that very reason I was shown mercy so that in me, the worst of sinners, Christ Jesus might display his unlimited patience as an example for those would believe on him and receive eternal life" (1 Tim. 1:16).

Picture in your mind some truly patient people whom you know. Friends, family, coworkers. What do they have in common? Most likely, the patience they possess comes from a yielded heart; a yielding to God's plan and purpose for their lives. That is a holy, worshipful place to be. Seeing others through the eyes of Jesus—how patient is that!

No wonder Jesus highlights this trait of patience all throughout Scripture. He knows how badly we need it. How very comforting to realize that God is always close by. We can bring Him our heavy, unmanageable burdens and roll them onto his strong shoulders daily, patiently placing them into His care.

What seems like a delay in our plans is often God's determination to bring about His pattern in our lives. While we often may quote Romans 8:28 to soothe our impatience at not getting what we want, we forget to read further (v. 29) to find out God's program may be different than our own. How often we forget that God is much more concerned about our character, our Christlikeness, than He is our comfort. In our limited understanding, it is difficult to fathom that God is always at work in every detail of our lives, for our *good*. But we have the above promise of God that, even in the time of trouble, He is going to work out everything for our *good;* not our pleasure or prosperity or popularity, but for our good. He always wants what's best for us. The same God who parted the Red Sea for the Israelites is available to work powerful miracles in your heart today. Our awesome God who healed the sick and calmed the sea is faithful in the smallest details of your life today. He loves you for what you can be in Him.

PATIENCE LEAVES A LASTING LEGACY FOR ETERNITY

Impatient the other day in the waiting room at the beauty salon, I became jittery, tapped my fingers, and flipped magazine pages rather loudly. After all, I had rushed through major noon hour traffic to get there on time. Didn't she know that traffic was horrendous at that time of day?

Ugh! I knew what I had to do. (After all, I'd been composing this chapter on the secret of patience.)

Silently I confessed my impatient, needing-to-be-in-control spirit before God. Then, leaning way back in my chair until my head rested against the wall, I closed my eyes, savoring the moment. It wasn't long until I was actually dozing and jumped half out of my seat when I heard my name called.

People will see Jesus in us when we show them what true virtues of Christ are. We must always remember what is at stake with our behavior. God is constantly at work creating within us that godly influence He desires us to be. "Therefore, as God's chosen people, holy and dearly loved, clothe yourselves with compassion, kindness, humility, gentleness and patience" (Col. 3:12).

If I ever hope (and I do pray for the opportunity) to get a word of witness for Christ to my hairstylist, I'm going to first have to mirror his love before her. That day was a good reminder for me that true Christianity is conveyed in my responses to inconveniences. My ability to speak with her about anything spiritual could have been hindered greatly in the future and I didn't want that. We learn patience so that we are able to convey to others the same mercy God has shown to us.

Just when we snuggle down in the bed of self-righteous complacency, God always has a way of waking us up. He sends along uncertainties and unanticipated opportunities (gifts in disguise) so that we can then share His love with others. Tearing off the wrapping paper of unknown packages left at our heart's door can be frightening. But when our plans belong to God, we can rest assured that we can expect something marvelous, even while we're in a waiting room.

Getting angry won't change your circumstances. Neither will slogging through a cesspool of self-pity; that only gets you stuck in the miserable grim of darkness. When you kick the wall you only end up with a broken toe and a scuff on the wall!

The advice of the Lord is hard, but it makes so much sense: "Be still before the LORD and wait patiently for him" (Ps. 37:7). God often teaches us patience so that we will take the path most honoring to Him, not the path most pleasing to us. He cares about all the details of our lives because they are barometers of the condition of our hearts. Sometimes the best way to know God's will while in a waiting room period is to do nothing. Only wait. We've all heard the adage, "When in doubt, don't!" That's good advice. We may learn more about his will as we allow him to work out his will in his own timing. In the meantime, we wait.

Are you in God's waiting room today? Your name hasn't been called yet? Lean back. Savor a promise in God's Word. Rest in Him. Don't despair. The Lord is developing the beauty of a patient Christlikeness within you to display in His art gallery of eternity. Await His perfect timing. Don't spoil the imprint of His love on the portrait He's painting of your life. "He has made me dwell in darkness ... it is good to wait quietly for the salvation of the LORD" (Lam. 3:6, 26).

Consider the children of Israel. After letting them go, the cowardly Pharaoh changed his mind and sent his large army after them. They found themselves at a place that seemed to them the end of the road. As they looked to their left, there were mountains. As they looked to their right, the mountains stretched on to the horizon. Straight ahead were the vast waters of the Red Sea. In their weakness they began to grumble to Moses. "We should have stayed in Egypt. At least there we have food and a place to live." But God has a greater plan. From right out of nowhere God parted the Red Sea. Just in the nick of time. And they passed to safety on dry ground.

Consider 5,000 hungry souls seated on the shores of a lake. We all know that hot, hungry people are not very patient. Imagine their amazement when a young boy with a sheepish grin stepped forward with only two fish and five loaves of bread and before they could belch, all their tummies were full and there were twelve "to-go" baskets full of leftovers. In their weakness, Jesus found them and fed them both spiritually and physically.

Remember Daniel and the den full of lions? God saw to it that those jaws locked until Daniel was lifted out. And once again, He did it in just the right time.

Don't forget David out on the hillside. He thought he would tend sheep for the rest of his life. Patiently, he sang to them and fought the wild animals that threatened to harm his lambs. God's plan was for him to be the greatest king of Israel.

What is it, in this season of your life, that your heart hungers for? Wait on God. He may not come when you want Him, but He'll be there right on time offering hope, healing, and grace even when we've impatiently lost our way. At the right time, His glorious plan will be made clear and the world around you will see Jesus through you.

That's His promise—so don't give up; don't doubt God's love for you. He has heard your prayers and knows your heart. Hold on to your faith one more day. Keep your eyes on Jesus; be encouraged. His answer is a whisper away. He's always an on-time God.

PERSEVERANCE

A GIFTed woman recognizes that she cannot choose life's circumstances, but she can respond with strength, stamina, and a staying PERSEVERANCE.

Two frogs fell into a can of cream,
Or so I've heard it told;
The sides of the can were shiny and steep,
The cream was deep and cold.
"Oh, what's the use?" croaked No. 1
"'Tis fate; no help's around.
Goodbye, my friends! Goodbye, sad world!"
And weeping still, he drowned.
But, No. 2, of sterner stuff,
Dog-paddled in surprise
As he wiped his creamy face
And dried his creamy eyes.

"I'll swim awhile, at least," he said—
Or so I've heard he said;
"It really wouldn't help the world
If one more frog were dead."
An hour or two he kicked and swam,
Not once he stopped to mutter,
But kicked and kicked and swam and kicked,
Then hopped out, via butter!

While not very theological, this story by an unknown author exemplifies tenacious persistence. Number one frog gave up. "What's the use?" was his life motto. He stopped swimming.

He drowned.

Frog number two had the motto, "I'll give it my best shot. I'll try." He kept going longer than he ever dreamed possible. Frog number two acknowledged the deep waters into which he'd fallen. Determined and with a tenacious resolve to make it, he kept swimming. He didn't let himself get distracted, but kept kicking and kicking.

He survived.

As a little child, was there ever a disappointing Christmas when you didn't get what you'd asked for? You know, you were expecting a bright, shiny red bicycle and what you opened was underwear and socks. That's not what you thought would be under the tree.

Whatever were your parents thinking?

Like a child on Christmas morning, we may be tempted to pout, sulk, or throw a feet-kicking, fist-pounding fit when life doesn't play out as we expected. After all, what was God thinking? Matthew 7:11 assures us that our Father in heaven knows how to give good gifts. But, because He is an all-wise, all-knowing, all-loving God, He doesn't always give us what we ask for.

God often overrules our requests. Rather than giving us what we want, He gives us what we need, or what we really and truly want, but don't even know to ask for. God's gifts always meet our needs. Could this be the secret to perseverance? Knowing that God never makes mistakes? One very important ingredient to persevering through all of life's unwanted and wanted gifts is letting the truth of Psalm 16:5 grip our soul: "LORD, you have assigned me my portion and my cup; you have made my lot secure."

God has assigned you and me our "portion." Into our life's cup He pours what He chooses. He pours factors over which we have no control. My particular "portion" includes my being born to Christian parents in the United States, female, the second daughter, sanguine personality, green eyes, fair complexion and hair. I had no choice in any of the above nor in many other givens—they are my portion assigned to me by God.

In a very real sense, then, my *portion* is poured into my life, my *cup*. My cup has included my birth mother dying when I was young, being then raised by my new mother who married my birth father two years later. My cup includes times of great financial difficulty, of being a "P.K." (preacher's kid), of moving around a lot and seldom attending the same school two years in a row until middle school.

Like a child shrinking back from a nasty tasting medicine, sometimes I've wanted to drink as little as possible from the cup God holds before me. I've questioned His methods and not wanted to drink from the bitter cup. Can you identify?

God assigned a bitter tasting cup to Jeremiah to the extent that he lamented, "I remember my affliction and my wandering, the bitterness and the gall. I well remember them, and my soul is downcast within me" (Lam. 3:19–20). Well, yes! Wouldn't your soul be downcast, downtrodden, after drinking from the cup God handed Jeremiah? After all, that whole chapter is filled with the bitterness of Jeremiah's cup given to him by God including:

- darkness rather than light (Lam. 3:2)
- broken bones, skin and flesh made old (v. 4)
- bitterness and hardship (v. 5)
- imprisonment—weighted down with chains (v. 7)
- prayers shut out (v. 8)
- left mangled and without help (v. 11)
- made to be the object of ridicule (v. 14)
- broken teeth (v. 16)
- no peace (v. 17)
- prosperity taken away (v. 17)
- splendor taken away (v. 18)
- all hope taken away! (v. 18)

Quite a cup, filled with quite a list! The weeping prophet had cause to weep. The Lord had assigned this prophet his portion just as He assigns you and me our portions. Jeremiah learned many lessons in perseverance.

THE SECRET OF SURVIVAL

This chapter on perseverance follows the secret about patience for a reason. Perseverance is the natural byproduct of a patient, waiting heart. Consumed with this thought these past few months, I've been praying "Lord, don't ever let me talk (or write) beyond my walk." It seems as though the underlying message of what God is teaching me presently is that I am to be steadfast, resolved, determined, resolute, not to give up, *to persevere,* no matter what methods of stripping away life's supports God pours in my cup in order that I might learn to trust in Him alone. God wants all of our hearts. Not half of our heart, or all of it sometimes; He wants it all, all of the time.

With my praying I'm also asking, "God, I'm yours, what do you want me to do?" He clearly keeps placing the answer upon my heart, "Hold on, hold out, persevere in serving Me—come what may; but most importantly, I want you to know Me. Keep your eyes, Sharon, on Me and who I *am* rather than what I can *do* for you."

When Rob and I first got married—over thirty years ago now—we were gushy, dramatic, and romantically demonstrative with expressions of our love. If you were to ask me if our love is the same now as when I walked down the aisle in a flowing satin and lace gown with mantilla veil, I would without hesitation say, "No! I thought I could not love Rob more on that day, but really, now I see that I didn't really know what love was all about."

The love that Rob and I share now day to day is much deeper, much stronger than our newlywed love. Do we still get gushy, share moonlit drives, red roses, and romantic, candlelight dinners? Of course—I married a romantic. We don't ever want to lose those touches to our love, but it's just that we don't *need* such dramatic displays as often. We are assured of each other's secure, steady love because we've persevered through some pretty dark days. Not very dramatic, but true.

That's the loving closeness God wants us to experience while drinking from life's cup. Himself. No matter what experiences fill our cups to the brim, remember that He is faithful and in the process of engineering circumstances through which He can reveal Himself in a deeper way to each of us.

God's faithfulness does not always take the form of deliverance *from* pain and adversity. Sometimes He demonstrates His deep love *through filling our cup with adversity.* Sometimes there's just no other way. God is no less faithful when filling those cups than He is when He fills some days with ease.

I cannot tell you how many women I've spoken with about this very issue. Many have lived in rebellion toward God for years. God did not do things the way *they* thought he should, so they wrote Him off as unfaithful and unloving, then turned their backs and walked away. Nowhere, however, in the Bible did God promise always to work things out the way we think He should. I'm convinced that many of us refuse to drink from the cup God has for us. We turn away and pour our own.

Case in point: Let's go back to Jeremiah. Jeremiah drank fully from God's cup. It was bitter, but he did not close his lips. He drank fully. Thus Jeremiah did not end chapter 3 of Lamentations with his lamenting and wailing. No, he had learned the tremendous secret of persevering—how to hang in there, no matter what, even when he witnessed the destruction of Jerusalem. Such a great loss, but read on to learn the secret of survival.

Take a moment right now to turn to Lamentations 3; read verses 22–38. Jeremiah begins by remembering what he knows to be true. What blessings Jeremiah now lists! By an act of his will, bad as things were, Jeremiah remembered that God is good. He then lists:

- God loves us (v. 22)
- seek God with our whole heart, soul, and strength (vv. 24–25)
- returned hope (v. 25)
- wait for however long it takes for God to act (v. 26)
- see God work in our lives (v. 32)
- God is in control (v. 37)
- God is great (vv. 37–38)

Thank you, Jeremiah, for helping the scales to drop from our spiritual eyes. We see now more clearly God's intense love for us. The very things we would not wish on anyone often become what draw us to Him. Can you trace the hand of God through His stripping away of support systems, finances, health—multiple trials to be fashioned more like the Master? Resolve to persevere. Lest we ever think the Christian life is a ho-hum, dull life—read on. Consider the stories of present-day believers whose lives went almost instantly from carefree and comfortable to a crash-course in intense perseverance building.

REAL WORLD EXAMPLES IMPACTING ETERNITY

God uses life experiences not to make us comfortable, but to conform us to His image. One of the reasons we have to *get* that truth is because life goes by faster than we can imagine. Before we know it, we've missed out on enjoying so many wonderful things because we save them for a special occasion or our "Sunday best." We all know family or friends who never use many of their beautiful dishes or furniture because that special occasion just never seems to come.

May we not let that happen! There is nothing like the real thing—living life to the fullest. May we determine to live our lives on purpose every day to make eternity count. I doubt if anyone sets out to live a life of irrelevance. Deep down I believe everybody would like to think that their lives contributed positively to someone else's existence. Sometimes it is a smile or a kind word that literally changes someone's day—or a life.

So let's go for it! Use your finest china today or someday soon. Take that throw off the couch and let the family sit on it.

The Home-going of Bill Hyde

When my daughter Melissa and I arrived at the airport in Singapore in March 2003 we were met by my sister and brother-in-law who have been missionaries in Asia for over thirty years. Painfully, they began to tell us the events that had taken place just six hours before our arrival. A bomb had just gone off at the airport in Davao, Philippines. Three hours after the terrorist bomb tore through an outer airport waiting area, Bill Hyde, longtime missionary friend of Keith and Suzanne, went home to his heavenly Father. Until March 4, 2003, no one even thought of this area as a target for a terrorist group. Davao City was considered a very safe place on the island of Mindanao.

Lyn Hyde is now beginning a new chapter in her life as a widow. She went through untold anguish in the aftermath of the bombing. By the time Lyn arrived at the hospital, over 100 victims literally were strewn everywhere. I hold in my hand at this writing a Filipino newspaper with a large color picture of two injured children sharing a hospital bed after the massive explosion. I am unable to describe the scene and sadness. Twelve people were working on Bill when Lyn first saw him. He was given one percent chance survival at that time. He did not survive.

"From December until Bill's death, the Lord also gifted me with memories of what seemed a perfect marriage. Each day as Bill and I worked together in ministry, prayed together, played together, and simply enjoyed being together, I would often think, 'Lord, can it get any better than this?'" Lyn writes in her e-mail newsletter to friends.

On Lyn's way to the hospital where Bill had been taken after the blast, she rode in a vehicle filled with missionaries and Filipino church friends. God brought the words of Genesis 50:20 to her mind: "You intended to harm me, but God intended it for good to accomplish what is now being done, the saving of many lives." She spoke them aloud to everyone in the car.

"I believe," Lyn continued writing, "that this was and continues to be God's promise to me. That as a result of Bill's violent death there will be far more Filipinos who will obtain eternal salvation through Jesus Christ than if Bill had continued working eleven- to twelve-hour days, seven days a week, until he reached sixty-five." (Bill had turned fifty-nine one month earlier.)

The most frequent question Lyn now hears is, "What are your plans?" Her answer: "I do not know. I do know that I can claim Jeremiah 29:11 for my life. However, at this point in time, the Lord has not given me any direction. It has always been my privilege to be called to serve the Lord in a foreign country. God has not removed that call to missions from my heart. From the earliest days of my life as a believer in the Lord Jesus Christ, all I ever really wanted to be was a missionary. I have surrendered the *what, when and where of my life to the Sovereign Lord.*"

What a spirit of perseverance! God continues to wipe away Lyn's every tear in her loneliness without her precious Bill. How can she get through her dark days? Because God is a faithful and good God. He is the all-powerful Sovereign of the universe. Nothing is too hard for Him.

TEENS WHO COUNTED THE COST

As difficult as it is to grasp, God was in Columbine High School on April 20, 1999. Two young women whose lives ended that day continue to make a difference because of their faith. Rachel Joy Scott was a compellingly honest girl who wanted to make a difference, who wanted her life to matter for Christ. This seventeen-year-old beauty was described as "funny, dramatic, charming, engaging, bright, upbeat, and charming." Beth Nimmo and Debra Klingsporn, compilers of Rachel's journal entries, had this to say, "When Rachel walked into a room, something *changed.* She was like a power charge. Rachel made things come to life."[12]

In Rachel's now published journals, we find her spiritual journey in her own words. My life has been challenged by her entries and I encourage you to read her diary of faith. She wrote,

> Well, March 5, 1993 is one of those *remember* days for me ... I didn't intend to do it. I didn't really decide to do it. I just slowly walked down the aisle till I reached the front (of the church).... That night, I gave my life to Jesus. That night I said yes to God.... The decision I made that night started a chain reaction in my life— and it was the best decision I ever made.

It was in the Columbine library that another beautiful teen, Cassie Bernall, faced her moment of truth. With a gun pointed at her face, her killer asked her to choose between her old life and her new life in Christ with the question, "Do you believe in God?" She took a deep breath, then answered in a clear voice, "Yes!"

"Why?" screamed the gunman. But he didn't give Cassie a chance to answer. He pulled the trigger and ended her life on this earth.

What would we have answered in that moment? What strength this youth showed at a moment of crisis. Cassie is with her Savior for eternity—nothing can take that from her. She had enjoyed long talks with the Lord about where she stood with Him. In her personal journals she writes of wanting to give her whole life to Him after she accepted Christ as Savior:

> Now I have given up on everything else—I found

it to be the only way to know Christ and to experience the mighty power that brought Him to life again, and to find out what it really means to suffer and to die with Him. So, whatever it takes, I will be one who lives in the fresh newness of life of those who are alive from the dead.[13]

How challenging to me it is that Cassie stood up for God with her "Yes!" The good news is that many, many teens all over the world are coming to know Christ through the powerful testimonies of these Columbine deaths. That they died is staggering—young, beautiful, their whole lives seemingly ahead of them. But, more important than their deaths, let it be known in no uncertain terms, are their lives. Lives that persevered even in death and accomplished God's purpose for the kingdom. In other words, these deaths were allowed by God. That's a hard sentence to write—much less believe. But we must.

THE STORY OF HEATHER MERCER AND DAYNA CURRY

At this writing it has been almost two years after the miraculous release of Heather Mercer and Dayna Curry from a Taliban prison in Afghanistan, but I am still amazed at how God has revolutionized my faith in Him through their story. These two lovely young women and six other aid workers were arrested on November 15, 2001 for sharing their faith in a Muslim land. Dayna and Heather (even without her mother's support) longed to go back to the country where they ironically claim they experienced the "greatest sense of freedom ever."

Listening personally to their testimonies at a women's

conference not long ago and watching their exuberant smiles, my heart was challenged to be ever-faithful where God places me. Heather says, "I know it's never going to be okay with my mom that I live this way, but in Matthew 10:37, Jesus said, 'Anyone who loves his father or mother more than me is not worthy of me; anyone who loves his son or daughter more than me is not worthy of me; and anyone who does not take up his cross and follow me is not worthy of me.' Although I love my mom very much, I felt that in the midst of all this, God was saying, I've still called you. This isn't a reason for you not to live out what I've told you to do."

So Heather went to Afghanistan—and true, she did not know that her worst fears might come to pass, but she persevered even though she wound up in prison for sharing her faith. Seemingly as normal as you or I, both Dayna and Heather developed a heart for God's kingdom and radically surrendered to work *wherever and however.*

Heather continues, "I had no experience to qualify me— only average abilities. In prayer I felt God ask me if I could do three things: *Can you love your neighbor? Can you serve the poor? Can you weep for the poor and broken people?* I came to see that God didn't need someone with extraordinary gifts and achievements. He just needed someone who could love, share her life, and feel for others as he did."[14]

To that I say "Amen!" *When God allows adversity to touch our lives it is often to equip us to love others.* Persevere. Let these stories of other women just like you be of great encouragement. I want to refer to one more lovely young woman having an eternal impact through her perseverance.

LISA BEAMER'S PERSEVERANCE OF FAITH

September 11, 2001 marks the day that changed Lisa Beamer's life forever. Her husband, Todd, hero of Flight 93, left this world with the now-famous phrase, "Let's Roll!" as he and other passengers overpowered terrorist hijackers, preventing an attack on Washington, D.C. Lisa's faith in the Romans 8:28 promise gives hope to others who lost loved ones on September 11 when she says, "My relationship with God through Jesus has been the *driving force* in my life.... Never has this been more precious to me than in the days since September 11."[15]

Several months after her husband's death, Lisa gave birth to her third child, a daughter whom Todd will never know this side of heaven, Lisa's object every day is to maintain perspective in raising her children. Does she get lonely? Yes. Are some days bathed in grief? Of course. But, even in the struggles of the daily life, Lisa's deep desire is that her children and others who hear Todd's story will arrive at a deep, real faith in God. "I don't want them to have head knowledge that God is good; I want them to know it in their *hearts.*"

One of the key verses that Lisa was studying in her Bible study the week prior to September 11 was Romans 11:34, a quote from Isaiah 40:13: "Who has known the mind of the Lord? Or who has been his counselor?" Lisa is thankful that this passage was the memory verse in her study on the Book of Esther that week. It was the very verse that helped her deal with her dad's death from an aneurysm when she was fifteen. Having this truth in the forefront of her mind obviously helped her through that week. She clung to it when she was prone to get angry or to ask, "Why us?" or "What if?" God knew on September 10 what would take place on September 11 and could have stopped it. In that way, Lisa finds strength in trusting in God's ultimate purpose for her life —"to know and to love Him better and to help others do the same."

Now, Lisa asks God to give her people whom she can see are different today because of Todd's story of faith in Christ. With honesty and fervor she states, "I'm here to do what God wants me to do and say what He wants me to say. As long as that's my objective, whatever happens, happens. It's really not about me or my plans or anything else." Wow. I do not know Lisa personally, but her faith in God challenges me to persevere through anything I may go through and I hope it does you, too. As I pen this chapter my heart is touched at what she and her children have already endured for Christ's sake. She's making her pain available to God for Him to use so that each of us may think, *If God could sustain her through that, I don't have anything to worry about.*

HAVE THINE OWN WAY, LORD

What examples of persevering faith these contemporary, real-life stories are to me. We see how God engineers circumstances through which He can reveal Himself and perform His plan. These, as well as our own personal testimonies, yours and mine, bear witness to the fact that in times of adversity we can come to a greater realization of what it means to persevere for Christ's sake.

Paul's "secret," as he referred to it in Philippians, was

his relationship with Christ. He discovered that true and lasting resolve in serving Christ was found in his deepening relationship with Christ. He discovered that placing his *all* in the hands of his Lord brought him great satisfaction (see 2 Corinthians 5:9). The goal of Paul's life was to please his Lord. He persevered even when things got difficult, demanding, wearisome, and inconvenient. I think it is safe to say that the following verses support that statement as he lists the perils he faced in his attempt to spread the Gospel:

> Five times I received from the Jews the forty lashes minus one. Three times I was beaten with rods, once I was stoned, three times I was shipwrecked, I spent a night and a day in the open sea, I have been constantly on the move. I have been in danger from rivers, in danger from bandits, in danger from my own countrymen, in danger from Gentiles; in danger in the city, in danger in the country, in danger at sea; and in danger from false brothers. I have labored and toiled and have often gone without sleep; I have known hunger and thirst and have often gone without food; I have been cold and naked. Besides everything else, I face daily the pressure of my concern for all the churches. (2 Cor. 11:24–28)

Having experienced all that, Paul perseveres and is still able to say:

> But he said to me, "My grace is
> sufficient for you, for my power is
> made perfect in weakness." Therefore

I will boast all the more gladly about
my weaknesses, so that Christ's power
may rest on me. (2 Cor. 12:9–10)

You see, it's all about the kingdom of Christ going forward. Paul echoes the same idea in his letter to the Philippian believers when he says, "I want you to know, brothers, that what has happened to me has really served to advance the gospel" (Phil. 1:12). Paul understood that his purpose in life was to bring glory to God by preaching the Gospel of Christ. Therefore, anything that happened to him in the process of obeying God was really for Christ's sake. In that sense, he makes it sound simple. By the time he wrote the Corinthian letters he had assimilated this secret into his lifestyle. It's just like watching a professional tennis match. After viewing players hitting the ball back and forth on television the other day, I wanted to go out and buy a racket. They made it look so simple. What I didn't see was the hours and hours of practice they had gone through before they ever stepped out on the court.

As we read the life of Paul, we see him at the end of a lifetime of learning. His life was full of extreme suffering, but he persevered for the Lord. What we see before us is what is possible if we press on. *If God can sustain him through all that, we don't have anything to worry about.* Our responsibility is to submit to the lordship of Christ, taking the words of a hymn of old and making them our prayer:

Have Thine own way, Lord.
Have Thine own way;
Thou art the potter; I am the clay.

Mold me and make me, after Thy will;
While I am waiting, yielded and still.
Adelaide A. Pollard

God wants to know if we are willing to give that which we love to Himself, our loving and living God who loves us so. What do you need to hand over into God's hands today?

PLACING YOUR ALL IN GOD'S HANDS

My human tendency is to want to reject the ordeal of deep and prolonged grief, or walking through a "fire," not to mention any ordeal such as the contemporary life experiences you've just read. Friends, let us pray that each one of us will be willing to accept *any* tool in the Master's hand that is molding us and shaping us into His image. The hands that were pierced for you hold the cup of His choosing to your lips.

Your sphere of influence may not be a Taliban prison cell or instant widowhood from a terrorist tragedy. But, for today, you and I need to gain strength in our Lord to keep on; to persevere by remembering, as Jeremiah did, that God is good. Knowing that assures us that we can place anything and anyone into His good, loving hands. In God's hands, anything and anyone is secure. Let's see what God's hands are like.

God's hands are full of majesty and power.

When Habakkuk had a vision of God, this is what he saw: "His glory covered the heavens and his praise filled the earth. His splendor was like the sunrise; rays flashed from his hand, where his power was hidden" (Hab. 3:3–4).

Isaiah heard God say, "Who has measured the waters in the hollow of his hand, or with the breadth of his hand marked off the heavens?" and, "My own hand laid the foundations of the earth, and my right hand spread out the heavens; when I summon them, they all stand up together" (Isa. 40:12; 48:13).

David said it this way: "Your arm is endued with power; your hand is strong, your right hand exalted" (Ps. 89:13).

God's hands are outstretched toward you.

God is always reaching toward you. God's hand will come right down where you are to hold you. God sees and understands when you need Him to do so. So outstretched toward us are the Savior's loving hands, in a sweet relationship—not unlike the potter with the clay forming a vessel of *his* choosing and a masterpiece of his plan. "But now, O LORD, You are our Father, we are the clay and You our potter; and all of us are the work of your hand" (Isa. 64:8 NASB).

We must not lose sight that the outstretched, strong hands of God are able to hold whatever heaviness we might place within them. As the old ballad says, "He's got the whole world in His hands." He does!

God's hands are compassionate.

Our loving Savior is today, just as in days of old, pleading, with outstretched hands that were scarred to save, for you to come to Him. He woos us to Himself. He longs to see that we persevere. He beckons, "Leave it in my hands."

Jesus laid His hands on the eyes of the blind, and they saw; on the ears of the deaf, and they heard; on the lives of leprosy victims, and they became whole; on the bodies of the dead, and they lived again; on little children, and they became the symbol of the way to enter His kingdom.

So gentle and caressing was Jesus' touch that He cured a

child's illness no physician had been able to alleviate. The girl's mother in Matthew 15 was desperate; the hand of Jesus gave hope. God is always willing to give us a hand if we'll just reach out to Him.

Do you think that *your* situation is stretching your faith to the very limits of your being at times? The secret to perseverance is placing your life in God's hands. Let go completely. Taking God's outstretched hand, you'll find out that together you can walk through any fire. It is not human resolve or gritting our teeth but placing our trust in Christ that helps us endure. Lay aside any weights that hinder you from running your race for Christ. Lay them where? Place them in His hands.

We can trust the One who died for us to take good care of us. We are to come willingly before Him and present ourselves to Him being confident that "He who began a good work in you will carry it on to completion" (Phil. 1:6).

CRUCIFIED WITH CHRIST

Some of us are content with our sins forgiven and a paid ticket to heaven. Therefore we never persevere in storms or truly know the fully resurrected life that comes from dying to self. Being crucified with Christ means that I have no more claims on my daily life. Identifying with His death means that I fully surrender to His will and not mine because I turned over my life to the Christ who frees us, invades us with His life and power. That is when the cross of surrender truly becomes an honor instead of a burden. Consider the words of an anonymous Civil War soldier:

I asked God for strength, that I might achieve,

I was made weak, that I might learn humbly to obey.

I asked for health, that I might do greater things,

I was given infirmity, that I might do better things,

I asked for riches, that I might be happy,

I was given poverty, that I might be wise.

I asked for power, that I might gain the praise of men,

I was given weakness, that I might feel the need of God.

I asked for all things, that I might enjoy life,

I was given life, that I might enjoy all things.

I got nothing that I asked for—but everything I had hoped for.

Almost despite myself, my unspoken prayers were answered.

I am, among all men, most richly blessed.

Does God have a plan for the immortal soul which He forms into being, adopts into His family, and seals "in Christ Jesus"? God has a perfect purpose and a plan for you, His own in Christ Jesus. He will reveal His plan through our faith that perseveres even when it's difficult.

IN SEASONS OF SURRENDER

Visualize your life as a beautiful mosaic—God setting each stone in place beautifully, one at a time. Don't miss out on one glorious stone—whatever it is that you're going through, persevere—for His eternal glory. Persevere during the difficult times. Persevere on days when life is *very* ordinary.

Live your life. Persevere in the life *you* are to live. Even if your story is not reported on the evening news or captured on the cover of a magazine, in your own way let your world know that you were here. Persevere. Take God at his Word. Open your hands and your heart wide and embrace the cup God holds before you. It's all right to ask Him, "Father, if there's *any way* you can get me out of this, please do!" (Jesus did in the garden of Gethsemane). Or as my mentor of over thirty years, Norma Gillming, said to me one afternoon, "Sharon, sometimes when you're in tribulation, it's okay to tribulate!" During a major season of surrender in my heart, God had been shaping my character to match my calling and I *so* needed to hear that.

Can you feel the Savior's arms around you today, my friend? Lay down that carefully-planned life agenda you have held on to for so long. Accept what God has for you in all of its goodness and all of its badness. Inspire others in both. Impact eternity by making somebody feel as though she is the most important person in the world today. Leave your mark.

Our loving Savior stands with outstretched, pleading hands to receive anything you present to Him in this season of surrender. By His tender mercies, stand fast; you're being fashioned more like the Master.

I assure you, on many days I've wanted to give up. On those days, I picture God's arms around me—remarkably, they are around you, too. He's whispering in our ears, "Never give up, never give up, never give up."

God doesn't give up on any of us, so don't you dare give up on yourself. Perseverance pays off!

SECRET Eight

PERSPECTIVES

∞

A GIFTed woman intentionally involves and invests her life in future generations by passing on godly PERSPECTIVES to the younger women in her world.

Your personal trials and triumphs become your special platform to make a difference in someone's life.

"Yoo-hoo, Sharon," I heard someone sing out the melodic greeting as I bent over to jerk another weed from my flower garden. *Oh, great. Who could this be? Here I am with sweat running down my face in my ragged cut-offs; looking awful and smelling worse. It's probably a church member and I'll have to be all nice to her or something.* Relieved, I turned to see my friend Stephanie bounding around the corner of our house waving her right hand.

"Hey, girlfriend. Could you use a break?"

In her left hand Stephanie held up a pint of my all-time favorite ice cream, Ben & Jerry's Cherry Garcia. I have this "thing" for Cherry Garcia. A big thing. Oh my goodness. Creamy clouds of ice cream with intermittent chunks of dark chocolate and ripe cherries, it's simply the best lick-your-lips-and-savor-every-bite flavor. On occasion, I've actually been known to ceremoniously consume an entire pint at one sitting. (Okay, I confess; on *many* occasions I've been known to do so.)

That kind of a break I could use. I quickly put down my spade.

Going from the bright sunlight into my dimly lit kitchen blinded me, but only temporarily. It didn't keep me from finding a spoon and I soon sat as still as a statue at my kitchen table with Stephanie. The only sign of life was a hand-to-mouth movement. Ah, I'd gone to glory, enthusiastically devouring the full contents of the carton. Stephanie needed to talk. While she chatted, I ate.

Sound irrational and unreasonable? Believe me, it wasn't. What you've just read was behavior befitting good friends, one young and one older. For several years Stephanie and I had developed and maintained a growing bond that brought great joy and blessing to us both. Mentoring moments like this one at my kitchen table were not unusual between us. God ordained this younger-woman relationship we have shared for several years. Unofficially, I've been the mentor, Stephanie the "mentoree." It's been an extremely rewarding, fulfilling friendship of passing on spiritual principles and truths as well as day-to-day life lessons for both of us.

"BE JESUS WITH SKIN ON"

As I've studied Titus 2 in the Bible and listened for God's direction as to how I could best carry out this passage, I've been guided by the words I heard a speaker say many years ago: "To influence other women, you become Jesus with skin on to them." Being a "Titus 2 woman" is being a spiritual mother to a woman younger than you. It's being available for God to use you with the gifts He has given you to share. It's encouraging, giving wisdom, sharing perspective, and cheering rather than criticizing. It's loving. I'm sure you can tell by the introduction to this chapter that I feel it's one of the most blessed relationships to be involved in whether you're on the giving or receiving end.

It's all about what women want and need from other godly women. They want an older woman to look up to. They want love and affirmation from a woman who's "been there" that says, "I know how you feel, I have felt that way before, and here's what I've found works to help me through." That's God's Titus 2 design—older women giving of their gifts to younger women struggling with the challenges of life which we have already faced. It is so important because God commands that we do so:

> Likewise, teach the older women to be reverent in the way they live, not to be slanderers or addicted to much wine, but to teach what is good. Then they can train the younger women to love their husbands and children, to be self-controlled and pure, to be busy at home, to be kind, and to be subject to their husbands, so that no one will malign the word of God....

It teaches us to say "No" to ungodliness and worldly passions, and to live self-controlled, upright and godly lives in this present age (Titus 2: 3–5, 12).

Surely you can find at least one woman in your life who is younger than you, no matter what your present age. May this chapter be a challenge to you to find some young woman to pour your life into and become a teacher in the classroom of her heart. What a joy it is to be a channel of God's love, guidance, and biblical perspectives. It is such a privilege to laugh with her, cry with her, to listen, and yes, to eat ice cream together. If you share this sweet relationship with a younger sister in the Lord, you will have done great things toward passing on to the next generation the truths of God's love, having set her on a path to live a life that pleases Him.

I know firsthand how God uses older women to train younger women in the areas of godliness, marriage, homemaking, and mothering. How thankful I am to the Lord for the women in my life who have passed on principles of how to live for His kingdom to me down through the years. As I look back, I can see clearly how God put specific women into my life, just when I needed them, to model before me and teach me hands-on ways to help with the nuts and bolts of living as a Christian woman. You, my fellow woman, undoubtedly have someone in mind right now whose name God has laid on your heart. She might need you to come alongside her.

How and Where to Reach Out

I am certain that wherever you live, God has a young woman just waiting for you to mentor—in your church, neighborhood, Bible study, or where you work. She may be younger in age chronologically or younger in years knowing the Lord. Remember, if you are twenty-five years old, sixteen year olds are looking up to you. Personally, I remember a sixteen-year-old young woman I knew when I was around ten or eleven. To me, she was the model of Christian womanhood—sweet, outgoing, loving, friendly. She was a godly girl who paid attention to me and that made a big impression on my heart. I thought of her as an older woman, a role model. I didn't even know the word mentor, but indeed that is what she was to me. I remember that she saw potential in me I would have never seen in myself. One day she pulled me over to the piano to sing with her. At my young age, that was a "biggie" to me. Her belief in me gave me the courage to pursue singing in church a few years later. It is only as I look back that I can see how God in His mercy and love gave me a number of older women throughout my life who greatly influenced me in very specific talents which I developed in my adult years to use for the Lord.

I know the first step on any new undertaking always seems the hardest. But God will bless when in obedience you step out in faith and trust Him to do the rest. Remember, you don't have to "have it all together" to help your younger woman face the challenges of her world. Just let her into your life and intentionally become a part of hers.

First pray, and then, pray some more. Cover this new ministry in prayer asking God to guide you, use you, and to lead you to some young woman with whom you can share your life experiences and your heart. Don't be afraid! The young gal won't bite! Knowing the Lord is at your side, go boldly before Him and ask Him to help you to become the woman He designed you to be—then, that He will allow you to pour your life into another's. Acknowledge your awareness of inadequacy, but don't let it be an excuse. When Moses was called by God he answered, "But, who am I, Lord?" God said back to him, "It doesn't matter who you are or what you are not. I am sending you." Here's a prayer to get you started in your own Titus 2 ministry:

Lord, use me to touch the lives of other women for Your glory. Show me what You want me to do and what action You want me to take in serving you. Guide my steps toward young women who need what I have to offer and give me opportunities to minister Your life to those around me. Lord, give me a generous heart. A heart that is willing to give, not just receive. Reveal to me who it is that you want me to specifically extend my hand to at this time. Fill me with love for her. Make her open and receptive to Your voice through me. Show me ways I can communicate Your love in a way that will be clearly perceived. Enable me to touch her with Your love today. Amen

Find great comfort in knowing that you do not have to be perfect. You don't have to begin with a "12-step program of mentoring." No, not at all. Keep it simple. The simpler, the better. Just let God lead. When God calls, He will empower. Just say to Him, "Here am I, Lord, send me." If you will just be available, God will show you that you have much to offer.

TRUE, YOUNG WOMEN CAN BE INTIMIDATING

Yes, young women in the twenty-first century can be intimidating. They are educated, high-energy, powerful, strong, and sophisticated. But they don't have what you have as an older woman. You have experience, a history of stories to tell about facing difficult situations and finding the answers that helped you make it through. That's a lot to offer! A young woman needs an older woman in her life to feel her deep pain and to point her to her Maker and to His heart of compassion. God wants to do just that, through *you*. Remember the words of the psalmist:

> One generation will commend your works to another; they will tell of your mighty acts. They will speak of the glorious splendor of your majesty, and I will meditate on your wonderful works. They will tell of the power of your awesome works, and I will proclaim your great deeds. They will celebrate your abundant goodness and joyfully sing of your righteousness (Ps. 145: 4–7).

The words of Scripture are strong words. They beckon, no, they compellingly command us to respond to God's call. Ask any young woman in her twenties or thirties how she's faring. If she is honest, with apprehension, she will say (as my young friend said to me with her voice trembling) "So badly we just want older women to tell us we'll *make it* and to offer a shoulder to lay our heads on to find encouragement and hope."

Celebrate! You Have That to Offer!

There you go—you're qualified. You have experiences and you have a shoulder! You see, when we look at mentoring from this perspective, it's already sounding easier and better than you expected. As older women, we have already found answers to the questions younger women are asking. Fear not, be assured, you don't have to be uncertain or wondering if you are "qualified." The answers are found in God's Word and in His Son. The fact that Christ dwells within us enables us to be a guide to those younger than ourselves. You don't have to have a Ph.D. or a seminary degree. You're a growing-in-Christ woman. You've walked through valleys and the mountaintops of life with Him. Honey, you bet you're qualified!

You see, what younger women need is not someone with an impressive resume or someone who will help them "find themselves." No, they need a woman who will help them find God. A woman whose life pleases and glorifies Him. They need a vibrant, pure, contagious, spiritual woman devoted to God. That kind of mentoring is best communicated not through a sermon or book, but through a life lived right out in front of them. That means an intentional, planned, one-on-one personal relationship over time. Now, that's what I'd call a walking, talking, living, breathing sermon.

Yes, we "older-than-somebody" women have much to offer the generations coming behind us. Paul realized that when he penned the challenge in Titus 2. You see, the "older women" who had raised their children in Crete were now gathering together in the afternoons under the shade trees after their work was done to gossip. (The equivalent of today's gathering at the coffee shop. Or at the mall. Or talking on cell phones in our cars.) Paul exhorts Titus that Christian women should be doing far different things as they grew older in their faith. He taught that the older woman was to show by her very example God's desires for a godly woman to be: temperate, chaste, respectful, giving, patient, cheerful, reverent, and communicating love in her behavior.

Rise above all the excuses the enemy may be filling your head with right now, like, "I'm not good enough. I have nothing to offer this younger generation. I'm too tired. I'm too busy. I've not arrived yet in my Christian walk. I'm outdated, obsolete. Someone might criticize. My relationship with my husband and children is not so good. Sounds like a huge responsibility. These twenty-somethings don't want to bother with me."

Don't let those fears keep you from what God wants you to do. If we are going to serve God with our whole hearts, we must be willing to stand apart from the crowd—and yes, sometimes that puts us in a very vulnerable position. The question is not "Will I be a good mentor?" But "God, how is it that I can obey you in this command?" The answer is easier than you may think.

HEARING GOD'S VOICE AND STEPPING FORWARD

Say "Yes!" to God. Step forward and be willing to follow God's leading in ministering to those young women around you. A key ingredient of a good mentor is that she is not afraid of being a good leader. "The secret of Andrew Carnegie's genius for developing others was his ability to encourage good qualities while holding fault-finding to a minimum," states John Maxwell. What a great observation. Thus, I whole-heartedly believe that a good mentor is an encouraging leader.

A mentor friend of mine in Florida, Donna Janney, defines the qualities of women in leadership with an acrostic that goes like this:

L—Listen
E—Eyes on Christ
A—Accountability
D—Disciplined Life
E—Encouraging Words
R—Responsibility
S—Servant
H—Humility
I—Integrity
P—Passion

Great qualities. They spell it out very clearly. Mentoring is a leading ministry of multiplication—a transferring of God's perspectives in your heart to the heart of your mentoree. Don't worry about teaching what you're not or what you don't know—just teach what you do know and who *you* are. There are times when younger women come to me who need more help than I am qualified to give. I steer them to the Word, a pastor, or a qualified counselor. But usually young women just need someone to listen, to remind them of God's truths, and sometimes to suggest a different or practical approach to a situation.

It may be that God will open a door with someone you

never dreamed possible—when you least expect it. I'll never forget the time Connie arrived at my door sobbing uncontrollably. I took her in my arms, held her, and just let her cry. We bypassed our scheduled walk and sipped coffee all morning at my kitchen table. After Connie described the hurts she was experiencing, I simply reaffirmed her for the direction God was leading in the decision she knew she had to make. We prayed and placed it all in God's hands. Connie found out that day that God hurts with us when we hurt. It was good to have an older woman come alongside when her hurts ran deep.

I want to ask you, Is God God? Is God good? Is God good enough? Is God good enough to help you carry out the command of Titus 2? Yes, and again I say a hearty "Yes!" in answer to each of those questions. The young women of the twenty-first century may look like they have it all together on the outside, but many are falling apart on the inside. It is time we older women stepped up to the plate and let them know, "You are not alone. You will make it." Tearful young women will be relieved to find out that they are not the only ones in the world to have fears, disappointments, and experiences they cannot handle very well.

Go ahead, you lead the way. Begin by asking God to lead you to a younger woman. We are not to force ourselves on others (God doesn't), but take some common sense steps to make a connection. You won't have to look very far. At church, pray for the young women who sit around you. Help out in the nursery and meet young mothers. Go to your pastor and shock him by volunteering to teach a

Sunday school class for young adults or offer to begin a Bible study. Ask any of the other teachers if they know a young woman who has a teachable spirit who could use someone to walk alongside her.

Don't wait for the younger woman to take the initiative. When I began a "mentoring-fellowship" group on Monday evenings in my home, I heard virtually from every young woman, "I was hoping you'd do something like this so we could get to know one another better." It may be a little awkward at first, but break the ice by presenting yourself available through something you both have in common.

Other ideas might be:

Have a video night in your home.

Learn something new together.

Write an encouraging note or send a card to initiate the friendship.

Jump in and help the younger woman with a job.

Take a meal or offer childcare.

Treat her to coffee or a tea-room lunch.

Schedule one night of Bible study or scrapbooking in your home.

Compliment the younger woman on progress she's making in some area.

Don't just "do church" with the women there on Sundays. Do "life" with them. Paul put it this way: "We loved you so much that we were delighted to share with you not only the gospel of God but our lives as well, because you had become so dear to us" (1 Thess. 2:8).

WELCOMING A YOUNGER WOMAN INTO YOUR HEART AND YOUR HOME

It's so much easier to feel like you know someone when you've been in her home. Let that be a training ground for mentoring. The most cherished mentorees I have ever been privileged to have in my home are my two now adult daughters. Both Missy and Mindy have made it very clear to me as young women now entering their thirties that they appreciate the support and strength I have been in their lives. From time to time, not just holidays, they often let me know how my mentoring them as their birth mother and as their spiritual mother has enabled them to become the women they are today. All right, if I keep going I'm going to need a handkerchief!

My point is, we should never push away our own daughters in the least little ways for the opportunity to nurture other young women God sends our way. I've known Bible teachers who will not open up their lives to their own daughters, but they are there right at the podium every time a Bible class needs a teacher. When your own natural daughter feels insecure in your love for her, that is not the time to be rounding up mentorees because you "have so much knowledge to share." If my Titus 2 ministering makes my two daughters feel pushed aside and that I have no time for them, it is time to step back. I never want to jeopardize my precious relationship with them and neither do you with your daughters.

My mother continues to this day to pour her life into mine long distance. Though the miles between us are many because we live several states apart, she mentors me with a grace and warmth that I appreciate more than words could ever say. I have the confidence that she will love me to the ends of the earth. Even so, I certainly don't want to endanger our sweet relationship. My heart is open to many women who teach me many things, but I would never try to "replace" Mother with one of them.

Do keep the right perspective on family ties—they are too dear to risk. When your family is secure and enthusiastic about your ministry with others outside the immediate family, they will be assured that absolutely no other mentoring relationship with any other young woman will ever change your love for them. That's when they get behind you and can welcome the joys God allows along the way.

When you invite someone into your home, you honor her. Hospitality is very important to God's heart. He even says sometimes He sends "angels unaware" for us to open our homes to if needed. So put the teapot on and ask God to lead you to a young woman to share a cup around your table. It's an easy place to get to know one another as "real"—not just someone out in the world. You could invite your new friend into your home to learn a new skill together. Or explore a new Bible study at your table. See what awesome things God will do when two women come together like this. Be listening and watching. A perfect example of that comes to my mind: an older lady in our church years ago overheard me compliment her apple pie at a dinner. She came right over and told me how that it had been a family favorite passed down in their family for years. She had it mastered! Crust and all! So the next Thursday she called me up and said, "Sharon, come on over. I've got my rolling pin out and a big batch of Granny Smith apples waiting to be made into pie."

I went. We laughed, we floured, we cut elaborate designs on the crust. I learned how to make apple pie. Not "dump the can's contents into a frozen pie crust," mind you. I used real flour and a real pastry cloth and even one of those handy-dandy apple peeling gadgets that peels and even slices. Am I a master like Dee was? No. But now with every pie I make, I'm reminded of the morning spent in the humble kitchen of an older, wiser, experienced woman who welcomed me into her heart.

Stop by your new friend's home and help her fold laundry. You'll be amazed how many of a woman's problems have been solved over a laundry basket. Run errands for or with her. Help out with the kids and share what you've learned works and doesn't work so well. When a subject comes up, discuss it. Just show you care. Be "Jesus with skin on."

Think of three younger women with whom you could be or now are friends. Have you used your friendship for mentoring? Are you unselfishly and consistently opening your home for relationship building? Are you so wrapped up in your own life that you don't see opportunities for ministering His life to those around you? Is there any younger woman who could say that Christ has made a difference in her world because of you? Is your life bearing fruit?

You can at the least offer hospitality and pour a younger sister in Christ a glass of cool water.

Was your home growing up one of hospitality and of giving blessing? If not, change that. Open your door to your present house. Welcome people into your home and you'll be welcoming them into your heart.

MAKE THE CONNECTION BY ACCEPTING AND AFFIRMING

Another woman who welcomed me right into her heart is one who seemed to understand me right from our very first meeting. In retrospect, I can't honestly remember the very first time we actually met, but I remember as a freshman in college noticing an English professor and she just smiled at me. Really big. You can be sure I looked for that smile every time I passed her classroom. Our spirits just seemed to mesh. I knew she loved words and so did I! (Not many of my eighteen-year-old peers *got that* at all.) Even though I didn't have Mrs. Gillming as an instructor, I watched her and I liked what I saw. I saw that she was a perfect example of the way God surely thought English and speech should be taught and spoken. Straightforward, above board, candid, witty, confident, and calming are all words that I would use to describe Mrs. G, as she affectionately became known. Throughout my college years I continued to watch her. God used this faithful woman to live out before me (and hundreds of future ministry wives) a life of gracious stability, faithful productivity, powerful and humorous speaking ability, and most importantly, seeking only God's approval and not man's.

Mrs. Gillming was unaware that I was watching. Oh, but I was. Years after I left Bible college, I remembered what I'd seen when I was watching. God knew I'd need those specific life lessons modeled before me to help me become the person He'd called me to be. It was exactly what I needed for the next step in my life. At God-appointed times, our paths crossed again. Our husbands were on several ministry boards together. God placed Rob and me in a church with a large ministry and many responsibilities. I was glad I'd been watching all those years. I began to glean wisdom from Mrs. G's years of experience, calling her every so often or we'd share dinners together when we were in the same city. I hung on her every word. Down the years a bit, it was with great pride that I had the privilege of introducing Mrs. G to my ladies when she spoke for our large women's spring banquet.

Through the years Mrs. Gillming has done something else very smart. She has made sure that her mentorees don't cling to her or become overly dependent for affirmation. She makes certain we know that's God's role. When I experienced some rough waters a few years ago, who but Mrs. G was one of the first to call and encourage me not to falter in my faith? She reminded me, "God doesn't give up on you, Sharon, so don't you give up on Him." She prayed for me words that I've not forgotten, "Lord, give comfort. Sharon has suffered enough." When I lamented in exasperation to her over the phone, "I don't want be cynical ... and bitter ... and ugly." Mrs. G was there with firm reassurances, "You won't. You're *not* going to." She helped me get perspective and I will forever be grateful.

The godly attributes I've seen Mrs. G live out over the past thirty-two years have served me very well. I have been sharpened by this woman, taught, refined (still working on that one!), and challenged. I thank my heavenly Father for the gift of her one-of-a-kind grace and love. He knew just what He was doing when our paths crossed in my college hallway. Every woman needs a Mrs. G in her life!

By now, you may be asking, "But, how can I, just one woman, make a difference?" Read the following piece and you'll have your answer.

ONE

One song can spark a moment,
One flower can wake the dream.
One tree can start a forest,
One bird can herald spring.
One smile begins a friendship,
One handclasp lifts a soul.
One star can guide a ship at sea,
One word can frame the goal.
One vote can change a nation,
One sunbeam lights a room.
One candle wipes out darkness,
One laugh will conquer gloom.

One step must start each journey,
One word must start each prayer.
One hope will raise our spirits,
One touch can show you care.
One voice can speak with wisdom,
One heart can know what's true.
One life can make the difference,
You see, it's up to you!

(Anonymous)

Remember how I told you that my mentoring with Mrs. Gillming these thirty-plus years ago started with just one smile? Well, you *can* smile, can't you?

Be a Woman God Calls "Great"

It is my prayer that this chapter has been just the impetus you need to reach out—to be willing to intentionally involve and invest yourself in the lives of other women. I dare say there are women all around you in your community, church, and neighborhood crying out for a caring friend. As believers in Christ, we have that to offer. In these days of high mobility and fragmented nuclear families, there is a woman in your world who needs you.

May the Father bless the desire you have to be "great" for Him—to do and teach His commands. What better way is there to make a dynamic difference in eternity than to start giving away what you have received in your own journey as a woman of God? The happiest women I know are those who have invested their time on this earth in the lives of others. You just be you, drawing from your own God-given uniqueness. Model Christ. Model a godly woman's perspectives on love for her husband and children with purity and kindness. Think God's thoughts. Follow Christ's character, His commands, and His will. That is what young women need. Come on, let a younger woman into your life close enough to see who you are and what's inside.

PRIVILEGE

∞

A GIFTed woman focuses heavenward through the
PRIVILEGE of worshiping Jesus Christ.

*Blessings flow into our lives as we cultivate an intimate love
relationship with Christ through worship.*

Earlier today I chatted on the phone with each of my
married daughters. I told them both how much I love them,
how I appreciate them, and what each of them means to me.
They individually echoed back the same sentiments. I just
loved it. My daughters' words poured out to me were like
perfume spilling a loving fragrance across the phone lines.
Even though we each talk several times a week, I never grow
tired of communicating with them, nor of hearing Missy and
Mindy's voices.

It is that way because we are family, and because we have

a wonderful long-term love relationship with one another. We just love to meet together to express our love.

Living as far from one another as we three do, you can be sure our phone lines are busy! No matter what my day's schedule holds, I am always eager to stop what I'm doing to accept a call from one of my girls. My deep affection, devotion, and love as a mother for each of them compels me to be in their presence as often as is possible, even if it is just by way of the telephone. It's how our relationship stays dear, fresh, close.

God wants us to be close in our relationship with Him by choosing to spend intimate time with Him in worship. When God called His people out of Egypt and they began to wander in the wilderness, He wanted them to set a place for worship to keep Him a priority in their lives. So important was this place of worship that God devoted eight chapters specifying all the standards, measurements, and furnishings that were all parts of the tabernacle (Exod. 25–32). Inside the tabernacle was the Holy of Holies, which held the ark of the covenant. On top of the ark was the mercy seat where once a year the high priest sprinkled blood as atonement for the people's sins. It was on this mercy seat that the visible evidence of God's glory "tabernacled," or made its dwelling.

Today, Christ's dwelling place is in the heart of the believer. Within your heart and mine God lavishes His love. "Yet a time is coming and has now come when the true worshipers will worship the Father in spirit and truth, for they are the kind of worshipers the Father seeks" (John 4:23). That is the very reason, in fact, that you and I were created. We were created so that God could literally take up residence within our hearts, and by doing so we would become worshipers of Him.

God longs for true worship to be the priority of our hearts. It is not to be an addendum to our day; it is to take precedence in all we do. Like King David throughout the psalms, we must purpose in our heart to seek to be a true worshiper. Many of the psalms speak of David's passion for worship. For instance, in Psalm 27:4 we are told of David's passion that was motivated by the love of God: "One thing I ask of the LORD, this is what I seek: that I may dwell in the house of the LORD all the days of my life."

There you have it. What does that verse reveal to us? David desired only one thing, that was all; but if he had this one priority, he knew all else would follow. The ruling passion of his life was not to be a great king, to be undefeated on the battlefield, or to be an incomparable songwriter. David's ardent desire was to behold, to feast upon the beauty of the Lord. That is true worship and in that worship David experienced an intimate fellowship with God that dominated his life. It is the person who makes the choice to put the "one thing" first that God chooses to share the innermost secrets of the His heart.

Have you experienced a time when you were so overwhelmed with God and His actions in your life that you just had to worship and praise Him? In a beautifully expressive portion of Scripture, 2 Samuel 7:18–29, David "went in and sat before the Lord." Listen carefully to the emotions that poured from his heart:

"Who am I, O Sovereign Lord, and what is my family, that you have brought me this far? And as if this were not enough in your sight, O Sovereign Lord, you have also spoken about the future of the house of your servant. Is this your usual way of dealing with man, O Sovereign Lord?" (vs. 18–19).

Have you ever felt as David did? Have you ever been so indescribably in awe of the blessings God has bestowed upon you and your family that all you could do was run as fast as you could and sit before Him? Moments like that bring me to my knees. I have asked the same question more times than I can count. "Who am I, O Sovereign Lord, and what is my family that you have brought us this far?" I stand overwhelmed at the goodness of God on our family's behalf at this season in my life. For reasons I will never understand this side of heaven, God has brought us further than I dared to imagine or dream. Some of the most wonderful things God has done are too personal and intimate to share in public testimony. They are moments that only God and I know. Nothing is quite like realizing the mystery of you and the God of the universe sharing intimate secrets. Every now and then, He reminds me of that fact, and I stand in awe like David:

"What more can David say to you? For you know your servant, O Sovereign Lord. For the sake of your word and according to your will, you have done this great thing and made it known to your servant. How great you are, O Sovereign Lord! There is no one like you, and there is no God but you, as we have heard with our own ears" (vs. 20–22).

So intimate were these words of David that he went from the presence of Nathan, the prophet, to be with God alone. There in private David thanked God for His unfailing love and goodness. It makes me want to shout "Hallelujah!" When was the last time you lovingly, intimately worshiped your Lord in private? Get down on your knees and ask Him to help you focus on Himself, not on your problems or circumstances. Before God and with all your senses today fix your eyes on Christ. You'll discover, like David, the many reasons you have to rejoice. If He is our focus, everything and everyone else pales in comparison. There is none worthy of our worship, no purpose, no power, no prestige, no possession, no purchase, no privilege, no priority, no person, except God alone.

THERE'S BUBBLING IN MY SOUL

Only as an adult have I come to understand the childhood chorus I used to sing in Sunday school. Today it would be called a praise chorus because the praise flows from a heart that just cannot contain the adoration of the Lord. As I recall, the song went something like this:

It's bubbling, it's bubbling, it's bubbling in my soul.
There's singing and laughing since Jesus made me whole.
Folks don't understand it,
Nor can I keep it quiet.
It's bubbling, bubbling, bubbling, bubbling,
Bubbling day and night!

I used to be in a dilemma about those words. Did the song represent a kettle on the stove bubbling over? As a little girl,

I just didn't get it. I do now—I think the composer wrote the little song not so much about joy in our hearts *from* God, but about praise and worship bubbling over *for* God.

When one's heart is so changed by the loving truths of God's Word and warmed by the confidence of His presence that it can't help but bubble over in praise, then that describes the true worshiper of God. Worship is the giving of "worth-ship" to the one you worship. Therefore, to worship is to divest ourselves of all desire to worship anything or anyone other than Jesus Christ. He and He alone is worthy of such praise and adoration. It just can't help but "bubble over." Once again in the psalms we read, "My heart is stirred by a noble theme as I recite my verses for the king: my tongue is the pen of a skillful writer" (Ps. 45:1).

"This is the day the Lord has made, let us rejoice and be glad in it" (Ps. 118:24). This passage does not say we are to worship and be glad if everything is zip-a-dee-doo-dah in la-la land. No, it says *"this day,"* no matter what happens, we can choose to worship and praise our Lord. Even during days when things are so utterly out of control that all I can do is throw up my hands and say, "I give up!" I can still be a faithful worshiper.

Today, Begin at the Beginning

One of the great thinkers of modern times, C. S. Lewis, became an authentic worshiper of Christ. "It is in the process of being worshiped that God communicates His presence to men," he wrote.[16]

Do you want God's presence to permeate your very

being? Place Christ on the throne of your heart and bow before Him as your Lord and Master. Do you wonder where to begin? Begin worship with knowing that the Lord Jesus loves us with all His heart. He desires that we in turn love Him with all of our hearts too. Unless we do, we cannot truly know the sweetness and depth of His precious love for us. We will only have a faint picture of His intimate love. There must be a response of love *from us* to His great love *for us.*

I came across the necessity to worship in my own life, as some would say, "quite by accident," though I know beyond a shadow of doubt that it was directly by God's leading. There was a day that I finally truly understood that my spiritual walk would progress no further unless I sought to worship the Lord. It was my birthday, October 31, 1999. I purposely planned a personal retreat in Daytona Beach, Florida after having spent a weekend speaking to women there. These twenty-four hours with Jesus proved to be one of the most special days of my life. The longest entry in all my journaling for over thirty-five years was on this day— eighteen pages. You can be sure I have received no better birthday gift before or since than this sweet time together with my Lord.

I began my day early by sitting on my room's balcony overlooking the ocean. It was one of those bright clear mornings that the Florida beaches are so famous for. The sound of the ocean waves tumbling over the sand and the seagulls singing far surpassed any distracting noise. As I began to read my Bible I acknowledged God's sovereign care and lordship over me. God created me, for "all things have been created through Him and for Him" (Col. 1:16 NASB). Being my birthday, this truth particularly drove home the fact that I was born at "such a time as this" for a reason far greater than I could have imagined. "You are worthy, our Lord and God, to receive glory and honor and power, for you created all things, and by your will they were created and have their being" (Rev. 4:11).

The King James Version uses the word "pleasure" in the last line of that verse, saying, "and for thy pleasure they are and were created." In essence both versions are the same. If I live for God's pleasure, I have done His will. I have accomplished the reason for which I was born if I'm bringing pleasure to my Lord. His lordship means His *total possession of me and my total submission to Him.* I began writing in my journal my heart's desires to, "lay aside the somber garments of fear and press onward to serve You, Father, in complete submission. I do not want to dishonor You by not yielding completely to You. I choose to let You alone, God, truly be the one and only God of my life. On this, my birthday, I want to live many *more years in grateful joy serving You than I did in rebellion and disobedience to You.*"

Continuing reading, God pressed His heart into mine through the love notes in Isaiah 43 (my personalization):

v. 1. This is what the Lord says—he who created you, Sharon, "Fear not ... I have called you by your name ... you are mine."

v. 2. When I pass through the deep waters, He will always be with me, and when I pass through the rivers they shall not sweep me away. When I walk through the fire, I will not get burned!

v. 3. For, He says, "I am the Lord your God.... your Savior."

v. 4. Since you, Sharon, are precious in my sight and honored.... loved!

v. 5. Do not be afraid, for I am with you.

v. 7. He created me for His glory!

v. 10. I am chosen as His servant!

Laying down my pen, Bible, and journal to go on a walk down the beach, I viewed the majestic, breathtaking ocean sights and sounds. I could scarcely contain the emotion and my mind began to fully comprehend the above verses in Isaiah as they continued to resonate in my heart. I knew what David meant when he said "such knowledge is too great for me."

As I walked on that beautiful beach, I said right out loud over and over, "O, Lord! Thank You for being my God!" And, guess what, He answered me! Not with an audible voice, but by bringing to my mind over and over the words, "I AM the Lord your God." Imagine that! The God who knows the very number of grains of sand upon which I was walking that day and with exquisite precision set the ocean in place—this same God is *my Lord and my God.*

I was having a hard time envisioning that. I guess it's true what someone once said, "If God were small enough to be understood, he would not be big enough to be worshiped." Immeasurably loved! Loved by the One whose majesty and power created the beach upon which I was walking—this very One was walking with me and talking with me and telling me I was His own, His beloved.

Singing praise choruses softly, I walked for miles. It was just Jesus and me, He holding me by His right hand. I thanked Him for pressing me in to His heart. I thanked Him for holding onto me, especially for the times when I let go. He never did. In between hymns and choruses I sang the great old song my daddy used to have our congregation stand and sing when he gave an invitation in our church, "I Surrender All." Tears flowed down my face when I came to the "… all to Jesus, I surrender, I surrender *all*." On far too many days in my life I have lived by the motto, "I surrender *some*."

Even today, as I think of that very special time a few years ago, tears of gratitude come to my eyes. Still walking and praying I found comfort in the conscious presence of my Lord. Strolling past folks eating their noonday meal, I felt not a pang of hunger. In the "lostness" of worship, He satisfied my soul. I caught glimpses of a mother sharing a drink of cool water with a child, but felt no thirst. The Fountain of Life had fulfilled my every need even to the point of physical fulfillment. I walked on—never alone.

I remember smiling at one point, watching a young couple embrace and speak in tender tones of their passion for one another. You could tell that love was on their mind. "*Mine, too*" I remember writing later in my journal, "*for today I am satisfied to know I have Your affection and you have mine.*"

Untiring, I walked on, still pouring out my dreams and hopes to Jesus—He never scoffed at one of them. The day ended with me thanking God for all the gifts He had bestowed upon me that day. I closed the day thankful to the point of glee, for my gifts, mostly for the gift of Himself and knowing how immeasurably loved I am. There is no selfish fickleness in love. I wanted to give a gift in return that day. Wrapped in love, I gave my worship, my self, and recommitted all the rest of my life to do my best for my Lord.

I had begun to know true worship.

THE HOW OF WORSHIP

It's time for you to begin the great gift exchange, where you take on the torch of worship carried by heroes of the faith. I discovered on my birthday that there are six characteristics of a woman who worships.

SOLITUDE. Come before a holy God in private (Matt. 6:6) regularly. Worship is regularly engaging in the privilege of meeting alone with your Savior in fellowship. Shutting the closet door behind you to meet in private aids in forgetting all else in order to meet with God. Then, and only then, can all your attention and affection be on the Lord, forgetting all else.

SILENCE. Wherever your closet might be (any closed off place from the world) your objective is quietness, listening to God's voice, not that of any other. A study of Matthew 6:6 shows that no less than eight times is the singular pronoun used, emphasizing how personal and intimate meeting with God in tranquility is to be.

SINCERITY. Come to Christ by way of the cross in brokenness. Catch a glimpse of Christ's amazing forgiveness, healing power, and love. Let His nail-pierced hands hold yours and lead you to the way everlasting. Permit His crimson blood to flow through your sin-stained life and wash clean all your shame and sin. Afterwards, you will be in an attitude of worship. Keep "short accounts," as D. L. Moody preached. Every evening before retiring he would review the day with his Lord, trusting Him to reveal anything that had displeased Him. With that done, when morning came Mr. Moody was ready to worship. An unclean heart forfeits access to God in worship. There can be no worship without obedience in confessing of sin. There must be clean hands and a clean heart.

SURRENDER. Putting no confidence in your self, but coming before God with dependence is submitted surrender. Come to God in worship with childlike simplicity, trust, and humility, realizing we must give up our rights. Pray, "You are God—and I am not!" That brings into sharp focus the primacy of worship. A GIFTed woman who longs to make a difference in her world reveres Jesus Christ as the Lord of her life. Then, we will be able to love life and love others as we seek the one who created us.

SCRIPTURE. Ascribe worth to Jesus through Scripture. Adapt verses that express how your heart feels and make them your own. For example, Revelation 5:12 is a good place to begin. Pray it back to God as follows: "You are worthy to receive power and wealth and wisdom and strength and honor and glory and praise!" The psalms, of course, abound with worship for the Lord. How would you make Psalm 104:1 a worshipful prayer? Perhaps something like,

"I bless You, wondrous Lord. I bless You. I bless You with all my soul, for You are my Lord and my God. You are very great."

Again, Psalm 91:1 could be,

"Lord, You alone do reign in majesty. You are clothed with strength and majesty."

Choose verses that completely occupy your mind upon God. I've adapted Psalm 139:1–4 for worshiping in this way:

"O Lord, You have searched me and known me. You know every-thing about me—my downsitting and my uprising, You alone under-stand my thoughts even when I do not. You guide my path as I walk through the day and my lying down at night. You are acquainted with all my ways. For there is not a word that I say or an action that I do, that You, O Lord, are not aware of. You know all things."

How beautiful to make the song of Mary, the mother of Jesus, a personalized prayer from your heart to God's heart (Luke 1:26–38):

> *"My soul glorifies the Lord*
> > *and my spirit rejoices in God my Savior.*
> *For He has been mindful*
> > *of the humble state of his servant.*
> *From now on all generations will call me blessed,*
> > *for the Mighty One has done great things for me—*
> *Holy is His name.*
> *His mercy extends to those who fear Him*
> > *from generation to generation."*

SINGING. Hymns and praise songs are a wonderful tool to aid us in worship. I have many traditional hymns hidden in my heart from childhood, but if you do not you can select a CD containing hymns of worship. Elisabeth Elliot says, "It is the old hymns that get you through the night." I do tend to revert back to them in my darkest hours, for they are intensely personal about our Lord.

> *Holy, Holy, Holy! Lord God Almighty!*
> *Early in the morning our song shall rise to Thee;*
> *Holy, Holy, Holy! Merciful and Mighty!*
> *God in three persons, blessed Trinity!*

Now, that is worship. Make the words your own. Memorize them and sing them in the car or softly while working. How pleasing to the Father's ears! Another worshipful favorite from my youth that seems to come to my mind often is:

> *Fairest Lord Jesus! Ruler of all nature,*
> *O, thou of God and man the Son!*
> *Thee will I cherish, Thee will I honor,*
> *Thou, my soul's glory, joy, and crown.*

Do you get it? Beginning to worship begins by actually beginning. By giving God the "worth-ship" He deserves. That doesn't sound very profound; it may be simple, but it is so true.

Remember the first time you saw the ocean? Or perhaps the Grand Canyon? Or held your firstborn child? You adored him and were in awe of every tiny thing about him! In wonder and filled with emotion let your wonderful God fill you with His wonder again—fresh and anew. Allow God to shower His great love on you today; adoration and worship will follow, I promise you. Isaiah 43:7 tells us that we were made for His glory. That is your ultimate purpose—to glorify the Father. It is awesome to know that you have been created for God's glory. Do you know that you are to live in such a way as to give all of creation a correct opinion of who God is? Give yourself time to meditate on Isaiah 43. There in awe you will find a peaceful contentment and rest for your soul in knowing the great design God has for you. He loves you that much. Thank Him, worship Him for that unfailing love.

Give God the opportunity to show you your great worth to Him. He will speak His love to your heart through his Word. Begin in the psalms—read them out loud. They are love letters to God written from the hearts of those just like you who love God. They will help you express your heart back to Him. Jesus waits for you to offer your praises to Him at the throne of grace so that He can intercede with the Father on your behalf. That's specifically why He lives at the right hand of the Father (Heb. 7:25). He longs to talk to his Father about *you*. He longs to tell Him that you are totally in love with Him and have purposed in your heart to be a worshiper of Him only.

How then, can you resist pouring out your fragrant worship? Set your will to make worship a priority in a consistent manner. I marvel at what a difference *choosing to worship* makes. Take a second look at Mary and Martha in Luke 10. Here we are introduced to two sisters who were preparing for Jesus to come to their home. We read earlier of how busy Martha was, but Mary was busy also. She was busy concentrating on a different form of service in preparation for Jesus' visit. Both sisters made a poignant choice that day. Jesus Christ was central in the life of Mary. There was a time when she had made that choice and Martha had not.

When Christ is central in the heart of a woman, what does she want to do? She wants to worship her Lord. She is compelled to spring into action. I don't mean the action of cleaning and cooking. Mary's passion led her to worship. I imagine she must have absolutely been overwhelmed with the reality that Jesus had come to her home. Long before Jesus arrived at her house Mary made the choice to sit at Jesus' feet. She knew what it was to have intimate fellowship with her Lord; she did not want to miss this, perhaps one last opportunity to show her devotion to him on this earth.

While Martha complained in self-pity, Mary worshiped. Note carefully Martha's attitude toward Jesus. It is so revealing of her heart, "Lord, don't you care that my sister has left me to serve alone? Poor me, nobody cares. Jesus, don't you care? Don't you see? I'm having to do everything. Mary isn't doing anything!" We see Martha's complaining spirit. If she complained to the Lord and rebuked even him, I wonder who else in the house was she in the habit of complaining to? Or bossing around. She even gave Jesus a command, "Tell her to come help me!" Whoa, now, Martha!

WORSHIP HIS NAMES

Worship is the outpouring of an awareness of who God is and His great love and believing that He is who he says He is and loves you as He says He does. Your worship time with

God will be transformed when you discover the limitless power of His name.

> Jehovah-Shammah—the Lord is present
> El Shaddai—Almighty God
> El Elyon—the Most High
> Jehovah-Jireh—the Lord will provide
> Adonai—Lords Master
> El Roi—The God Who Sees
> Jehovah-Rapha—The Lord Who Heals
> Jehovah-Shalom—The Lord Our Peace
> Jehovah-Raah—The Lord is my Shepherd[17]

It was the custom of Hebrew parents to name their children a name with significant meaning. The name "Jesus" is the watchword for the Christian here on earth and it shall be the password for anyone to enter into heaven: "Salvation is found in no one else, for there is no other name under heaven given to men by which we must be saved" (Acts 4:12). Our eternal hope rests in His name and we pray in His name (John 14:13). "O LORD, our Lord, how majestic is Your name in all the earth! You have set your glory above the heavens" (Ps. 8:1). His name is the only One truly worthy of our praise. There is none like Him. "The name of the Lord is a strong tower; the righteous run to it and are safe" (Prov. 18:10).

You are the only person who can fulfill the purpose for which God created you—you, a GIFTed woman, created to give God the honor He deserves. Look up. Look around. Engage with the majesty of the moment. Make room for worship. Find at least one reason for saying, "Ahhhhhhh," in awe and wonder of your Lord each and every day. Let your life, everything you do, be as an act of worship unto Him, 24/7. Become wonderstruck with God afresh and anew.

But, that's not all. Get into the habit of worship, for one day every creature in heaven, on earth and in the sea will sing: "To Him who sits on the throne and to the Lamb be praise and honor and glory and power, for ever and ever!" (Rev. 5:13).

You don't have to wait for that day to sing praise to the Lamb. He is worthy of your worship right now. From the overflow of a joyful heart, join in praise with your whole heart. Allow yourself to be so overwhelmed with the person of God and His actions in your life that you simply have to praise Him. Moments like these unlock the key to indescribable intimacy in your relationship with God. What a privilege to go in and kneel before Him. The privilege of worship—a precious secret!

SECRET Ten

PAST YOUR PAST

⌀

A GIFTed woman leaves the prisons of the PAST behind.

Those I love may not remember the words I say, but will never forget the life I've lived.

While growing up, my daughters shared a small bathroom near their bedrooms in the upstairs part of our home. The sounds coming from that bathroom down the hall in the morning before school were telltale signals of what kind of day it was going to be. Sometimes I'd hear the giggles and pleasant murmuring of two sisters doing whatever it is sisters do to get ready for school in the morning. Then, there were those *other* days.

"Did not!"

"Did too!"

"Did not!"

"Did too!"

191

About this time I would step in. "Girls, that's enough."

"Well, Missy started it!"

"I did not. Mindy did!"

"Did not!"

"Did too!"

And on it would go. If you've raised more than one child, you know the routine.

Nothing could ruin my first cup of coffee in the morning like those annoying sounds. Whether it was bickering over a curling iron, or someone else's sweater, or innumerable other annoyances, those sounds become obnoxious. And did it really matter enough to turn a shared mirror and bathroom sink into a battleground?

"Girls! Can't you get along?"

That's a good question for all of us to consider. Why *can't* we get along with one another? I don't know any responsible parent who overtly trains children to be cynical and selfish. Children seem to come by that quite naturally. At least mine did. "Mine!" appears to be one of the first words out of most toddlers' mouths. As squabbles begin, each child stingily thinks it is to be her toy, her doll, or her way.

Sadly, many children intensify their capacity for selfishness by watching adults. Strife, jealousy, hatred, spite, rivalry, resentment, envy. Time and time again adults have been poor examples of self-egos, self-fulfillment, and self-satisfaction. Women who grew up in the sixties heard over and over the seductive mantra to "do your own thing." In the New Testament, James asks us, "What causes fights and quarrels among you? Don't they come from your desires that battle within you?" Disappointingly for all of us, we find out that "doing your own thing" is a sad, unfulfilling way to live. We also find out that we cannot expect our children to do what we are not doing; nor to be what we are not being. That includes getting along.

WHAT IS THE WORD ON THE WORLD?

Me, myself, I—we do all get caught up in it. All too often I hear myself mentally screaming, "But they started it! It's not my fault!" or "I only went a little over the line!" Selfishness and worldliness often do not fall on a person like an avalanche. More often, it is a slow, steady drip, drip, drip that eventually wears away our resolve. Just a little smudge of dirt here, a little unnoticeable dust there, and before we know it, our lives are covered with the dirt and grime that only the world can produce.

This book is all about taking God's ways to heart so that we can be an influence to others. Our goal should not be to impress others with our "own thing" assertiveness, but to impact them with a selfless life lived for others. A GIFTed woman is less concerned with impressing others than with impacting others with godliness. One way we can do that is to encourage each other to stand strong in the areas of righteousness and purity. Who you and I really are is determined by what we do when no one else is around. Though I'm far from perfect—even weak and carnally minded at times—my sincere desire is to bring honor and praise to God—and to encourage you to do the same. Like you, I am a woman who wants to *seek* first the kingdom of God and His righteousness

(Matt. 6:33). Also like you, I have to be pointed to Jesus for grace and cleansing when I need forgiveness from my sin. We all are tempted, tried, and fail sometimes. Again, the New Testament is specific about our propensity to sin. "There is no one righteous, not even one; there is no one who understands, no one who seeks God. All have turned away, have together become worthless; there is no one who does good, not even one.... for all have sinned and fall short of the glory of God" (Rom. 3:10–12, 23). The same insidious dirt corrodes each of our hearts. Let's just call it what it is: sin.

During one of my father's pastorates when I was a young child my family lived in Joplin, Missouri in an apartment that was, well, suffice it to say, not in the best of conditions or in the most elite part of town. We'd return home from church at night, flip on the lights, and hear the pesky little cockroaches run in every direction. Those eerie little creatures only came out in the dark. Sin is so much like those nasty little bugs. When the light of God's Word shines brightly into the corners of our heart, the dark figurative demons of our hearts disappear. When we expose ourselves to the light, the light uncovers the dark places of our hearts. Our enemy does not want us to be changed by God's brilliant light.

Satan is our enemy.

This is not a game.

This is all-out war.

As you enter this battle, fling open the shutters of your heart and let the Light of God's Word shine in.

The Bible teaches us to live in this world, but not to partake of the evils of this world. The spiritually minded woman is not to "love the world or anything in the world" (1 John 2:15). John goes on to define the world we are not to love:

> For everything in the world—the cravings of sinful man, the lust of his eyes and the boasting of what he has and does—comes not from the Father but from the world. The world and its desires pass away, but the man who does the will of God lives forever (1 John 2:16–17).

In another instructive passage, Peter tells us, "Be self-controlled and alert. Your enemy the devil prowls around like a roaring lion looking for someone to devour" (1 Peter 5:8). Satan will create temptation in your heart when you least expect it. Selfish living will be marked by valleys of giving in to those temptations. Satan's desire is to keep us under his control so that we fail to bring God glory with our lives. To do so he uses temptations of every size, shape, and source to disillusion women into setting their sights on the things this world offers instead of things God offers. But you don't have to give in, and neither do I! We have the Holy Spirit, who lives within every believer, giving us the power to stand strong against the pull of sin. As we surrender and yield our wills to God, the Holy Spirit takes control of our lives. Paul specifically addressed this issue. Writing to those who professed a relationship with Christ, he said, "Since, then, you have been raised with Christ, set your hearts on things above, where Christ is seated at the right hand of God. Set your minds on things above, not on earthly things" (Col. 3:1–2).

God offers to us the power to withstand the enemy. As you read the following promise, give Him the praise for His protection in your life: "No temptation has seized you except what is common to man. And God is faithful; he will not let you be tempted beyond what you can bear. But when you are tempted, he will also provide a way out so that you can stand up under it" (1 Cor. 10:13).

SATAN'S DIRTY DOZEN

I have no way of knowing where you are in your spiritual journey at this moment. But I know that if you are walking and talking and breathing, Satan has declared war against you. I can only imagine what challenging temptations Satan and his gremlins have before you right now. What I do know by listening to women all across our country and in other nations as well is that he has his favorites.

I've listed his tactics as the "Dirty Dozen" in this chapter and the two that follow. These are Satan's ways of seducing a woman's heart. As you read through the list, remember— Satan wants you to become his victim through these destructive behaviors, but God specializes in victory. In Him, we can overcome and move past the past.

As you discover each of these destructive actions, identify which ones keep you from moving ahead in your spiritual journey. Be willing for God to bring conviction into your heart. Ask Him to bring into light a clear picture of any or all of them that are strongholds in your life. You may even find yourself surprised at areas the Holy Spirit reveals to you. Be honest with yourself and with God. Many are the women who fail in the quest for peace and happiness because they refuse to be honest with themselves concerning these activities.

Self-delusion is perhaps the most extravagant of sins.

Also remember to meditate on the passages of Scripture that I've presented with each of these Dirty Dozen. In the Word there is victory! As I've battled with the devil in many of these areas myself or walked beside other dear sisters in Christ as they've battled, I've learned a thing or two the hard way. I believe with all my heart that the Word of God brings freedom: "the truth will set you free." (John 8:32).

In the Word of God you will find grace and mercy in your time of need. Draw from the positive difference each verse or passage of Scripture can make in your heart. Oh, how we desperately need to be women of purity in this dark world. We must determine to live clean lives and stand clean before the Lord and humankind. Only then can we progress from defeat into victory.

Be tenacious as you go to battle against the Dirty Dozen. Be steadfast and unmovable! Be armed with the Truth. Hide God's Word in your heart. It is this Truth and this Love that will protect you, "For our struggle is not against flesh and blood, but against the rulers, against the authorities, against the powers of this dark world and against the spiritual forces of evil in the heavenly realms" (Eph. 6:12). While Satan is the captain, the dark forces of our enemy are made up of many soldiers. Notice that the words used to describe what you are up against are all plural:

Rulers—many!
Authorities—many!
Powers of this dark world—many!
Spiritual forces of evil—many!

Yes, Satan and his followers may be many, but don't forget: God is God! Before reading on, take this crash course in spiritual warfare so you're not caught off guard. I know what it is like to stumble, fall, and lose the battle. In times past I've tried to enter heated warfare with the enemy and I've ended up in defeat. Duped into thinking I could wage war without the proper armor, I was not equipped and was defeated miserably. The pain was tremendous and came with great personal cost. May we keep our eyes on our Captain and march forward in victory.

As we begin, pray this victory prayer:

Help me, God, as I go to battle, to stand firm with the belt of truth buckled tight around my waist. May I put on all the full armor of God, so that when the day of evil comes, I may be able to stand, and after the battle, still be standing.

Father God, tighten the breastplate of righteousness to guard my heart, with my feet wearing the confidence that comes with the gospel of peace.

I must stand being able to discern the enemy's tactics, protected by the shield of faith, with which I am protected from the flaming arrows of the evil one.

Mighty God, help me to take on the helmet of salvation, that my mind will detect deceit and not abandon You, my Savior.

Lord God, help me to hold on unswervingly to the sword of the Spirit, which is your true, holy Word of God.

I pray this now and always, making my requests

and supplications known unto You. My enemy longs to devour; I keep my eyes on You with all perseverance that Your peace will guard my heart and mind in Christ Jesus.

Reporting for duty. Ready for my marching orders, Sir.

Amen.

DIRTY DOZEN DART #1 — UNFORGIVENESS

I will give her the name Ann. At our church years ago, if I didn't see her, I just didn't feel like I had been to church. She was always there handing out bulletins and connecting with everyone. I rarely went a Sunday without a hug or a kiss on my cheek as she whooshed by. I became the recipient of many gifts from Ann and more compliments than I could ever tell you. Is it any wonder that I practically jumped out in the aisle to see her?

Then came the Sunday that I saw a look on Ann's face that I had not seen before. An "I'm never speaking to you again" look. Whoa! No matter how hard I tried to catch her that Sunday, I never could get close. Or the following Sunday. On Monday, I phoned—she did not answer. I sent a greeting card. Then another. I racked my brain to remember anything, *anything* that might have caused Ann's sudden change in responses to me.

After a two-week cooling off period, at last Ann called. She desperately needed me to drive her and her daughter to the doctor's office. No, I was not glad the little one had a tremendously high fever, but I was thankful that Ann's car was being repaired and she needed me for a ride. What a weight was lifted off my shoulders when tearfully Ann poured out what it was that had upset her so. There was no malicious intent on my part; and as we talked Ann began to see that she had misunderstood my actions. Ann forgave me when she realized that I, too, was appalled that such a simple issue could cause unintended injury. It has helped me forever to take into account that friends are always going to do unpredictable things, sometimes without thinking. At all times, I need to be ready with a gift of forgiveness.

Ann asked if I could stay for coffee. I could and I did. We picked up right where we left off and have an enduring friendship to this day.

Unforgiveness is emotionally, physically, and spiritually destructive. It may even be what is keeping you from experiencing God's love and forgiveness. I truly believe that a person who refuses to forgive is a person who stands to be hurt and harmed the most in life. If we do not forgive, we cannot experience God's forgiveness and we will not receive answers to our prayers. "And when you stand praying, if you hold anything against anyone, forgive him, so that your Father in heaven may forgive you your sins" (Mark 11:25).

How important the act of forgiving is! My ability to forgive those who have offended me even determines whether my prayers are answered or not. One lovely woman I recently met could not accept the love of her heavenly Father because she would not forgive her earthly father. "I hate him and I will not ever forgive him!" was her angry cry. This appalling emotion poisoned her relationship with God by eating away from within her ability to love Him. As we prayed and read God's Word together, I could see the Holy Spirit begin to soften her hardened heart. Finally, she said, "I do want to forgive him. Please, Lord, I want to forgive my father so I can be close to You."

God's clear command reads, "Be kind and compassionate to one another, forgiving each other, just as in Christ God forgave you" (Eph. 4:32). Forgiving those who have offended us is not an option the believer can choose, but a principle of obedience we must follow if we are going to be close to our heavenly Father.

Perhaps you have confused forgiveness with an endorsement of your offender's actions. God asks you to allow Him to deal with the offender in His way. One of the most practical words from God on the subject of forgiveness comes in Romans 12:17–19: "Do not repay anyone evil for evil. Be careful to do what is right in the eyes of everybody. If it is possible, as far as it depends on you, live at peace with everyone. Do not take revenge, my friends, but leave room for God's wrath, for it is written: 'It is mine to avenge; I will repay,' says the Lord."

Nor does God tell us that forgiving is forgetting. Some offenses cause scars so deep that forgetting is humanly impossible. God understands that we will not forget those often horrible things done to us. But He still commands us to release our offenders into His hands. By doing so we learn the real meaning of forgiveness, and we can experience love for someone that we really should hate. We are to forgive others because God has forgiven us. He commands us to forgive anyone who has wronged us in any way—whether they be brothers and sisters in Christ, or even an enemy. "Love your enemies, do good to those who hate you, bless those who curse you, pray for those who mistreat you" (Luke 6:27–28).

May I share with you some practical instruction on how to forgive? Like so many other things in our lives, I believe forgiveness is a *choice* we must make in order to follow Christ. Forgiveness is possible, but Satan sure doesn't want it to be true in our lives. I wandered far too long before learning to forgive others. I think now of a season in my life when I had been badly wronged. I didn't want to forget that those hurtful incidents happened. In fact, I relished in reliving them over and over. I deliberately would not let go because the persons said they were not sorry. So they did not deserve my forgiveness, right? After all, if I forgave, that might mean everybody would just go on through life okay. And I was not okay!

Months went by, and I was still not okay. Deep down, I hoped that my offenders were hurting too. I thought the offenses were too great for even God to forgive. But when I realized the toll it was taking on me and virtually every one of my relationships, especially with the Lord, I said, "Enough is enough! I'm tired of hurting and I'm ready to do something about it!"

I waited for directions from the Lord. As I did, He impressed upon my heart these promptings:

"Daughter, will you *love* me?"
"Daughter, will you *trust* me?"
"Daughter, will you *believe* me?"
"Daughter, will you *praise* me?"

As I began to let God work in my heart, He showed me the assignment he wanted me to undertake. The Holy Spirit convicted me of my sin and I confessed my weakness before the Lord. By an act of my will, I laid at His feet all my human desires to harbor unforgiveness. By doing so I turned a major bend in the road. My anger began to dissolve and deep peace filled the place where once bitterness had been. The precious penetrating peace can be yours also. As you choose to forgive, God will grant you a newfound joy. Forgiveness came when I surrendered my right to get even with the persons who had hurt me.

Will you surrender that right toward those who have offended or hurt you? This may be difficult, but God commands it. While forgiving others often requires time and is often very difficult, God *can* change attitudes and be victorious in the most difficult of situations. Jesus' answer to Peter's question, "Lord, how many times shall I forgive my brother when he sins against me? Up to seven times?" was "seventy-seven times" (Matt. 18:21–22). The clear teaching from Jesus is that we are to be ready and eager to forgive at all times.

Sometimes those who deserve it least need forgiveness the most. Forgive just as God forgives you. Leave the past behind. You'll be so glad you did. Your Father will be watching!

DIRTY DOZEN DART #2 — ANGER

What do you, as a Christian woman, do when you are betrayed or wronged? Get even? Get angry?

I have known some angry women down through the years. Just this past month I was confronted by one mighty angry woman who shook her finger in my face wildly—and whose vocabulary was just as wild. These kinds of women are not fun to be around for long. Watching them become paralyzed in their wrath has not been a pretty sight. They grow older and more resentful, hostile, bitter—certainly not the picture of dignity and grace we find in Proverbs 31.

I have heard all my life that Christians are not supposed to get angry. At the same time, I read in James 1:19 (NASB) that we are to be "*slow* to anger." Additionally, in Mark 3:5 Jesus "looked around at them in anger, and deeply distressed." There is a time and place for "righteous indignation." I call it anger. My conclusion is that the Bible does not forbid anger and displeasure, but we are admonished to not let our anger be in control of us.

Excessive anger is anger that is uncontrolled. It is marked by outbursts of temper and often the use of harsh language. It is demeaning, debilitating, and causes others harm. We must examine both the inner attitudes that drive us and the outer responses that identify our behavior. Anger may even be a response to someone's actions that God is using to refine our character and mold us into Christlikeness. Often we get angry when we see that we are not going to get our way, or when our rights have been somehow violated. When I take these hurts to God in prayer, I begin to realize that God is using circumstances and irritating people in my life to file off those rough edges and make me more like Him.

Anger may be considered a normal reaction to an incident when you and I are wronged, humiliated, and mistreated.

When approaching the subject, prayerfully consider this question: Am I under control when I am angry, or am I letting anger store up over time so that it gets dangerously out of hand? Many times anger is a matter of demanding our own rights—my things, my way! I know it sounds simplistic, but reducing problems to a practical level often helps me. Look at it this way: If Christ had demanded *His* rights, He would never have gone to the cross to suffer for our sins. They were not His sins, they were ours. He could have been considered the ultimate victim, but instead chose to be the overcoming Victor by yielding His rights. Once again, the New Testament tells the story in compelling form: "Your attitude should be the same as that of Christ Jesus: Who, being in very nature God, did not consider equality with God something to be grasped, but made himself nothing, taking the very nature of a servant.... And being found in appearance as a man, he humbled himself and became obedient to death—even death on a cross!" (Phil. 2:5–8).

Many irritations can make us angry. Some become prime opportunities for Satan to get a foothold in our lives. As believers, we need to make our anger a sincere matter of earnest prayer. Propel all that energy and effort you are currently putting into your anger and use it to energize your prayer life. By doing so you will receive such a blessing. What happens to the person who angers you so? Will he or she change? Maybe, maybe not. But *you will change*. That's what happened to me.

It was one very hot summer, and I'm not talking weather

here! For several months I poured out my anger and negative feelings concerning a very painful situation. I prayed earnestly, even journaling many of my prayers. It was a very hard time for me. Undoubtedly, many of you will identify. In my circumstances I wanted to obey God, but I also wanted to have my way. All summer long my body was drained of physical strength and my mind was clouded. In short, it was a real bummer of a summer.

As I write today here at my desk, I have my journal of that summer by my side. One daily journal entry reads, "My anger is preventing the process of forgiveness to take place. I cannot see the light at the end of this dark tunnel. Getting through each day is sheer torture. Please, God, forgive my present anger. I don't want to be this angry forever. I choose to thank You for this trial. Show me the purpose of this pain; I want to cooperate with whatever it is You are trying to do in my behalf."

God honored my humble efforts. In those months He worked a pure, unadulterated miracle in my hard heart. As the sun's rays softened into fall, my hard heart began to soften. Near the end of the summer I wrote this entry in my journal: "Admittedly, there have been moments that I thought these events would destroy me. I should not be surprised at your faithfulness, Lord. You have taken what others intended for evil, and used it all for my good. As the man stretched forth his withered hand, I have held out my withered heart to You. In quietness and confidence, You have been my strength and shield. I am not angry anymore."

Thanking God for even our pains and trials is a way we

let go of the anger and the past. Telling the Lord that our deepest desire is to cooperate with Him allows us to become free. Anger is often expressed toward people, but more often it is expressed toward God for the way He has ordered our lives. Sometimes we even do this without realizing it.

Pray that you will have a conscience void of offense before God and man. You will be glad you did. God's ways are not our ways. Aren't you glad? His way is so much better.

DIRTY DOZEN DART #3—A CRITICAL, NEGATIVE AND JUDGMENTAL SPIRIT

There are times as I move from day to day that I see and hear so much of the negative that I'm tempted to get caught up in it. Be honest with yourself. Don't you get caught up in it also? While some may have difficulty categorizing something so common as a critical spirit as sin, in reality, it is one of the most severe of sins because it can spread like a cancer and take over the heart. How many times have you heard, "If you can't say anything good about someone, don't say anything at all." Unfortunately, all of us know people who have the attitude, "If you don't have anything good to say, sit down right by me!"

There are three vitally important questions to ask before speaking about someone else. If each of our conversations were guided by these three questions, there would never be a hint of the negative in what we say.

Is this a *wise* thing to say?
Is this an *uplifting* thing to say?
Is this a *true* thing to say?

We have discussed how God's Word is to be the yardstick of our lives. We need to painstakingly align ourselves with the measurement that God uses. Our attitudes, appearances, and actions should be such that what we say and what we do is a beautiful display of all Jesus has done for us. God is very clear in His Word about how we speak of others. "We know that we have passed from death to life, because we love our brothers. Anyone who does not love remains in death" (1 John 3:14). "All men will know that you are my disciples, if you love one another (John 13:35).

I have found that it is impossible to love others if I am going to be constantly critical of them. Are you committed to loving others? That love pouring from your heart shows the pre-Christians around you that you have what they have been looking for—and that the love they see comes from Jesus Christ. The opposite is also true. Why would a woman who is seriously considering the claims of Jesus Christ be drawn to someone who claims to know Him, but who constantly finds fault with others and displays a negative spirit toward others in general?

Do you see the good in people or the bad? Do you build others up or put them down? The acid nature of criticism is hurtful to others and even to you internally. One of the best ways to relate to others in an accepting manner is to practice caring by "speaking the truth in love" (Eph. 4:15). Love is what turns things around. Love releases us from bitterness and a negative spirit. It is love that gives us the opportunity to make an eternal impact with our lives. Here is a little exercise that has been helpful to me and thousands of women. Put your name in the blanks below, and then read each line aloud.

_____ is patient,

_____ is kind,

_____ does not envy,

_____ does not boast,

_____ is not proud.

_____ is not rude.

_____ is not self-seeking,

_____ is not easily angered,

_____ keeps no record of wrongs.

_____ does not delight in evil

_____ rejoices with the truth.

_____ always protects,

_____ always trusts,

_____ always hopes,

_____ always perseveres.

_____ never fails.

(1 Cor. 13, adapted)

Love looks for the good in others. The enemy comes to steal and destroy love. We truly must be our constant guard to "do everything in love" (1 Cor. 16:14). Along with loving others, we must be alert to the devil's efforts to destroy love in our homes, churches, and relationships. "Show me your ways, O LORD, teach me your paths; guide me in your truth and teach me, for you are God my Savior, and my hope is in you all day long" (Ps. 25:4–5).

In a very practical way these verses instruct us in how to go down the path of truth. We are not always going to like the way other people do things, nor are we going to like everything they say. When we visualize the body of believers as God's family, we can understand that fragmentation and critical tearing down of one another must displease the Father. It hurt me as a parent to see my girls quarrel; how much more it must bring sadness to God when some of the children exclude and devour one another through such negative and critical speech. It tears apart any sense of kinship in the family of God.

You don't have to be in a position such as mine, performing on a platform, to have pride in your heart. Do you love people in your church? In your family? Do you love some more than others because they are rich or look nice? God can only do a great work in our hearts when we are willing to be honest with Him. One of the ugliest sins I ever have to confront is my critical spirit. It seems on some days, that every time I turn around I start fault-finding or judging others. God is faithful to bring to mind the ugly words and thoughts I have like, *"Who does she think she is? Why is that ministry being blessed instead of ours? I know as much as she does!"*

Just writing those admissions makes my heart feel like it has been smashed into many pieces. But I am thankful that when God is faithful to bring conviction, my heart does break. Not too long ago I fell before Him on my knees and verbalized what I knew was sin. Every word and every thought of criticism came pouring from my heart. They were sins hidden from others, but not from me, and certainly not hidden from God. I went to a person under God's leadership to say "I was wrong." Yes, it was petty, and yes, it was hard. But God gave me great personal relief for laying that burden down. I was free! I should have dealt with it a long time ago.

A simple, well-timed word of encouragement can have such a positive influence on a person. Before long it touches another, then another. Like concentric ripples caused by tossing a pebble in a body of water, the effects of encouraging words continue without stopping. In just a moment the pebble drops to the bottom, but the ripples continue on and on.

My prayer for myself is that I could be "God with skin on"—a safe place for others to come so they can pour their hearts out to someone who will listen without judging them. That is one of the most precious truths I know about God. He is our refuge where we can find compassion and love. I have met women before who will not come back to church because they feel others are condemning them, sitting in judgment of them, or making accusations against them. God wants us to be a refuge to others within our sphere of influence, a secure place of safety. If you're going to have friends, be a friend. And friendships often begin with a word of kindness.

From now on, before you chastise, judge, or criticize someone, ask yourself, "How does Jesus see this person?" If we will consider this question often, much of our criticism will cease. In Mark 14 we see the story of a woman who brought to Jesus her most prized possession, perfume valued at possibly a year's wages. But she did not just bring the perfume as a gift for Jesus. She opened the bottle and poured it at His feet, modeling one of the most beautiful pictures of worship in the entire New Testament. But the disciples did not see it this way and they began to criticize and judge her, protesting such a waste. "Some of those present were saying indignantly to one another, 'Why this waste of perfume? It could have been sold for more than a year's wages and the money given to the poor.' And they rebuked her harshly. 'Leave her alone,' said Jesus. 'Why are you bothering her? She has done a beautiful thing to me'" (Mark 14:4–6).

Jesus saw the entire event from a different perspective than the disciples. He even praised the woman for her actions. So before jumping to conclusions so quickly, as we often do, we need to see if Jesus might be approving of the other person's actions. Only God can see another person's heart. Let's give others the benefit of the doubt; even if it's not something just like we might do. Many a new believer has been discouraged to serve God at the hands of another believer's criticism.

In the New Testament, James says, "Everyone should be quick to listen, slow to speak" (James 1:19). The wise writer in Proverbs 18:21 says, "The tongue has the power of life and death." Let's choose life.

If we are going to "talk the talk," we are going to have to "walk the walk." Let's not make a mockery of our faith by saying one thing about God and his love, then not having a loving spirit toward others.

DIRTY DOZEN DART #4—DEPRESSION

I know firsthand how Satan robs women of peace and happiness through the terrible emotional and physical upheaval of depression. I hear it everywhere I go. It is one of Satan's finest and most well-aimed weapons. I allowed months of pain for myself because I did not put my faith in all of heaven's resources that were right at my disposal. I resisted truth. I resisted family and friends. I resisted help. For quite a long time I hid behind the excuse "I was just born this way."

Make no mistake about it. The pain of depression is very real, but I would not let myself *feel* it. Although I knew good and well that I was depressed, I did not want to admit it. That hurt too badly. Instead I threw myself into busyness. Especially early in our ministry and marriage, I punished myself for not doing enough. I would often push myself to give to others more and more of my emotional, spiritual, and physical strength. So much would go out of me that I had nothing left for my own heart and soul. My cup was bone dry, yet I still poured out to others. I believed the lie that I must perform to be worthy, loved, and accepted. Because of this I was not feeling God's unconditional love.

Physically, I found I could not keep up with Rob's pace, however hard I tried. I could not accept my own needs or acknowledge them even when loved ones were honest with me. So much of why I was depressed day after day was my own unrealistic expectations. I could not fulfill high expectations I placed upon myself. I experienced high and low mood extremes. Add to that the physical exhaustion, past unresolved grief from my birth mother's death, low self-esteem, guilty feelings, and too much to do.

Phew! I've probably got you depressed by now. But I want

you who are not prone to this malady to understand its very real pain. I didn't see it until it was too late. When I began to realize there indeed was help available to me and that other people besides me had survived depression, my pain began to ease. The first step in recovery was to go to a caring, Christian counselor who helped me assume personal responsibility for my attitudes and actions. He did not excuse everything away, just because "that's the way Sharon is."

With medical and spiritual guidance for several months, change for me was possible. I was encouraged to lay my life bare before God and confess my depression before God. The word "confess" means to "acknowledge or admit a fault or problem." It means to agree with God concerning my behavior. For far too long I had chosen to stay gloomy and was unwilling to accept God at His Word—unwilling to believe that He could exchange my depression for "a spirit of power, of love and of self-discipline" (2 Tim. 1:7). If you have a friend suffering clinical depression, remember the first step in recovery is to assume personal responsibility.

Notice I'm not saying that depression is a sin. I'm trying to be clear on that. But I have discovered that nowadays the battle is won or lost in my mind—or you may call it my will. If I choose to give up, to let my mind dwell on earthly things, then I simply am choosing not to win the battle. Only by turning to God's strength and grace can that be done.

Has your depression been a burden for you far too long? Would you like a fresh start? Surrender it to God. Go to the Christian pastor or professional counselor who can help you. Family and good friends are great, but they generally are not trained to help you deal with and correct the depression, especially when medical issues are involved and require treatment. The last thing we need is people who will just coddle us instead of pushing us to get help or frankly telling us the truth we need to hear. Brooding the past over and over won't help you move on either. When I read that Paul set a goal of forgetting the past—I see that I should, too.

Depression is nothing to be ashamed of. Please do not ignore ongoing feelings of utter hopelessness. You do not have to live that way as a believer. Your life can be redirected through Jesus Christ. As one who went from deep distress to joy in living, I know how magnificent it is to see the Lord work a miracle in a life.

I believe that God allowed me to experience depression not to defeat me, but so I would have a greater compassion for those who also battle it. I needed to learn how weak I am on my own. Depression was such a dark time that rendered me powerless—unable to fight. That's where Satan wanted me. And that's where he wants you. You might not think you are vulnerable or susceptible. Take heed! That's when we fall. Often after a major victory, the hole of depression is there to trap us. Be vigilant; beware, and be in the Word! Do not let the sun go down on your anger—anger turned inward causes depression. Sometimes that deep anger in depression goes so far as to make a person have suicidal tendencies. If you or a friend you know has suicidal tendencies, get spiritual professional help immediately.

Psalms 42 and 43 reveal some key aspects of the painful thinking patterns of depression. Learn to defeat depression and nurture your faith by letting the Word of God govern your life.

God wants you to be at peace and filled with His joy. Don't let Satan imprison you in his power—Christ can and will set you free.

Don't Miss the Best at the Last

This is quite a list! The Dirty Dozen Darts pierce deep into our souls. Like me, you may be needing a break in the action or you might miss some of the good stuff. We'll pause here a third of the way through, then finish the list in the next two chapters.

In this interval, I want to encourage you to continue on, though your heart may be aching from identifying deeply with some of the first four darts. I have a word of hope to offer before we finish. I don't want you to miss the best part.

During a retreat I attended two summers ago, I slipped away from the group at free time and headed out on a long walk alone. This steamy afternoon, I welcomed the trees that shaded the path as I climbed up the Colorado mountain. I began to sing songs of praise to the Lord at the top of my lungs. No one else but He and I were out on this mountain anyway.

What a sweet, refreshing time together we shared for several hours. Praising and praying, I "looked up to the hills from whence my help comes" (Ps. 121:1, paraphrased). Heaven never seemed closer. God used those verses and songs to convict my heart. I recommitted my heart and life to Him that day. "Anywhere, anytime, anything for You,

Lord." I prayed, I sang, I quoted verses aloud in adoration and worship unto my God. It truly was one of those mountaintop experiences that comes along once or twice in a lifetime.

Coming back down the mountain was slow going. After losing footing several times, my eyes pretty much stayed downward on the rocky path. Coming down was not nearly as inspiring as going up. My canopy of green became sparse and I grew hot and weary. Just moments before, I had been looking up into the heart of God. Now I was tired, my feet hurt, I was hot, and I wanted a drink. A cold shadow slipped over my spirit. All previous exhilaration disappeared. Life felt so very ordinary again.

Sitting down to rest, I removed my shoes and rubbed my feet. The Lord spoke firmly to my heart, "That's true. Life *is* ordinary. But, Sharon, you have an *extraordinary* God." I needed to be reminded. Sometimes I get so discouraged by how much *me* there is in me! I need to learn how to let God *be* God!

After a while, I resumed hiking down the mountain, and there! There it was—the most beautiful red-orange flower growing, of all places, out of a boulder. It was so unusual. Flowers don't grow out of rock; we all know that! I'm glad I wasn't looking down. Had I been, I would have missed it.

The Lord tenderly once again said to my heart, "That's true. Flowers don't ordinarily grow out of a rock. But Sharon, you have an *extraordinary* God." How true! Only God can make something beautiful grow out of rock … or a hardened heart.

God planted a special flower in a most unusual place to remind me of His great love for me. I don't believe it was there by accident. Neither are you. I extend my personal invitation to you, to join me in the remaining Dirty Dozen Darts. Go ahead—pour another cup of tea.

This Dirty Dozen list is birthed from my own experiences. Had I experienced a perfect life, I dare say I would not be in ministry to women today. When we focus on God's passionate, loving forgiveness, we are able to get past our past. Let that truth wash over your being. Though the Dirty Dozen list has us on a rough, steep uphill climb, there are treasures to be found all along the way. Jesus wants nothing more than to take you in His arms and reassure you of His forgiveness. He has no hidden agendas to make us pay for our sins. Oh, but keep your eyes up, not down. You're going to be amazed—and you won't want to miss a thing. There may be a special flower blooming just for you!

PURITY

∽

A GIFTed woman lives a life of PURITY based upon absolutes in God's Word.

But among you there must not be even a hint of sexual immorality, or of any kind of impurity, or of greed, because these are improper for God's holy people (Eph. 5:3)

Our next secret is not popular in the headlines of today's women's magazines. Yet it is a secret that impacts our hearts each and every day—the secret of godly purity. Satan whispers lies in your ear that purity and virtue are only for fools in the twenty-first century. He wants you to lose heart. Yet Satan himself is the ultimate fool and is only looking for other faithless fools to join him.

I remind you of the old saying: "Misery loves company." Mustering all the skill he possesses, Satan contrived a well-thought-out plan that deceives women into the sins of impurity. Many of us have bought his bill of goods and believed his lies. Shame is our result. Satan loves it. He bursts out laughing each time we rationalize: "Surely something that looks this good can't be bad for me. After all, something that feels so right can't be wrong. Can it?" or "Isn't it okay to experience the ultimate expression of love before I get married so I can know if we are compatible?"

Make no mistake, Satan has no new tricks up his sleeve. Just like Eve, many have let Satan's lies enter their minds, falling into sin's shameful grip. True beauty is born from a life of purity. You'll see how in these next four darts that focus on the many aspects of purity. Tough going for some, but the struggle will be worth it all.

DIRTY DOZEN DART #5—COMPULSIONS AND ADDICTIONS

"Run ragged." That's how I described my physical and emotional state when a friend phoned to ask how I was doing a few years ago. My words were a telltale signal to back off for awhile. I was in the exhausting aftermath following months of giving out more than I was taking in, both physically and spiritually. Yes, even ministering can become compulsive. There is always need; always one more person with whom to share Christ, one more dear woman who needs encouragement, or one more conference at which to speak. I had been invited by churches and the leadership of various groups and begun traveling where the Lord guided. It was brand-new territory for me and I was loving it. It was the fulfillment of a lifelong dream that had lain dormant in my heart for many years.

But ministry should never be a foot race or an idol. In my zeal to walk through the many doors it seemed God was opening, I ended up feeling like I was hanging in the air hazardously from a thin branch with nothing under my feet. I was about to crash. Backing off and spacing my travel according to what I and my family could handle realistically was a new challenge for me. I thought I could handle it all. But, where the Lord guides, He provides. Rob and I deliberately carved out specific times that I would minister out of town and specific times of oasis when I would back away for awhile. What a sense of relief!

God will be faithful to you, too, with whatever category you fall into today. While there may be psychological dynamics to work through, ultimate victory over patterns of compulsiveness rests in the spiritual power and control of the indwelling Holy Spirit in every believer. Nestled in the hearts of all of us are destructive behaviors, even within the heart of the most laid back of women. Human beings are selfish creatures, always seeking pleasure, which lies at the root of many compulsions.

Many of the things the world points us to for pleasure in fact bring us pain and lack of peace. Many women then quickly move to more pleasure-seeking places to eradicate the pain that life has brought upon them. Jesus speaks of this "world" in the New Testament. John writes, "Peace I leave with you; my peace I give you. I do not give to you as the world gives. Do not let your hearts be troubled and do not be afraid" (John 14:27).

John cautions against looking to the world for peace. He

knew firsthand that only God can give true and lasting peace. Not things, not shopping, not food, not drink, and certainly not drugs. In Bible times, drunkenness was not uncommon. Like today, many women used wine to alleviate the pain of being a slave, just a bearer of children, an object to service the men of that society.

But Jesus changed all that. He took the time to stretch out His hand and heal women in a time and place where those women needed him most. Many of those women were hopeless victims of a very male-dominated culture. In Christ these women found equality with men. "There is neither Jew nor Greek, slave nor free, male nor female, for you are all one in Christ Jesus" (Gal. 3:28). While sin had brought perversion and pain, in Christ there was to be a change in personal behavior and cultural practice. Victory and freedom were possible in every aspect of a woman's life for the first time in history.

Similarly, in the sophisticated American culture, there is freedom to be had, yet many who are reading these lines right now may choose to continue in secret addictions and indulgences. I meet women all the time whose "appetites" have become their masters and gods. These appetites leave them empty and unfulfilled. Enough is never quite enough! I suggest that when our focus is on anyone or anything to fill the hunger of our soul, our love and approval needs remain empty, filled only with the false promises and empty pretenses the current world system offers. The sad result of such false promises is a culture racked by anorexia, bulimia, gambling, substance abuse, and many other idols of compulsive behavior. This is no news flash to anyone, I'm sure.

I've spoken with women whose addictions or compulsions may sound strange to you, or compulsions may live deep within your own soul. It is important that you not underestimate the power of your enemy. He uses our television sets, magazines, computers, the clamor for attention, past pain—whatever it takes to greedily try to stuff our hearts and bodies full of pseudo-gratification. Women work themselves into exhaustion and believe that, even though the compulsion is tearing them apart, they must continue to work themselves silly.

I have a dear woman in mind whose days are spent popping pills and compulsive eating until she regurgitates so she can start the process again. She is a very attractive person who loves Christ and is very disturbed by her problem. She finds it hard to be a good sexual partner to her husband unless she overcomes her inhibitions by drinking to the point where she is able to endure the experience. It is difficult for her to stop smoking, and she pops a pill when her family complains that she cannot go more than a couple of hours without a cigarette. She shops incessantly, then is angered when her husband says there's no money left in the checkbook for more new clothes. She began taking drugs for back pain caused by a fall and now she is dependent upon them.

We can excuse ourselves by saying this woman is the extreme. Okay, but how about you and me? What habits and compulsions control us? When anything apart from the Lord Jesus Christ Himself controls us, we are sinning against Him. It is not God-honoring or healthy to live under the control of any substance, whether legal or illegal. This dear lady is seeking professional help from her pastor as well as a Christian counselor who is helping her deal with the psychological and spiritual root problems that drive her to bizarre behavior. There is no magic formula—but she is at least owning up to these fiery darts of the enemy thrown at her daily.

I often ask myself a question regarding control of my life. *Am I being controlled by anything or anyone other than Jesus Christ?* Am I overeating, oversleeping, overspending, overworking, over-anything?

It may be painful and difficult, but it is possible to maintain balance. The grace of God is freeing—you do not have to be in bondage to selfish desires, impulses, and passions. I encourage you to cultivate fellowship with spiritually minded women in a Bible-teaching church where you can be supported and be accountable to ever-encouraging believers.

> Do you not know that your body is a temple of the Holy Spirit, who is in you, whom you have received from God? You are not your own (1 Cor. 6:19).

> In the same way, count yourselves dead to sin but alive to God in Christ Jesus. Therefore do not let sin reign in your mortal body so that you obey its evil desires (Rom. 6:11–12).

Choose God's truth over Satan's lies! Seek Him with your whole heart. Ask Him to be your strength in your areas of weakness. One of my dearest friends in this world sent me the following words and with her permission, Kim and I together pray that they might encourage you in your struggle:

> She looks into the mirror and grimaces at her reflection.

She steps onto the scale and turns away in disgust.

She stares at the fashion magazines with bitter envy.

Do these scenarios seem all too familiar? Believe me, I understand. I, too, have fallen captive to these traps, which have induced self-hatred and low self-worth. As women, we are easily deceived into believing that our weight, looks, clothes, and social status will bring us fulfillment and satisfaction. But, my friends, it is a lie—a lie from Satan—the great deceiver. Satan knows women—he has studied them since the beginning of Creation. He knows how we are influenced and how to cripple our influence for Christ. If we insist on pursuing his lies we will live lonely, joyless, and unfulfilled lives. However, as daughters of God, we must understand that only Jesus Christ offers the true and lasting value and self-worth we seek. But it can only come when we deny our own will and determine to fix our eyes on Jesus and obey His Word. Once we die to ourselves we can begin to see ourselves as our heavenly Father sees us—precious and beautiful. His undying love and intense passion for us alone should fill us with delight and deep satisfaction.

Like you and like me, Kim is still on her journey. May we all encourage each other as she is doing on her path to healing and wholeness.

DIRTY DOZEN DART #6—SEXUAL IMPURITY

As I have traveled and spoken across our country, I am saddened by what I see. I have felt brokenhearted for the lack of purity of womanhood I see in our nation. So-called Christian America silently tolerates a twenty-first century

Sodom and Gomorrah. Too often we as Christian women are a stumbling block to the gospel because we will not live by God's standards. His clear teaching is that as his representatives on planet earth we are called to "be holy as He is holy."

Just as the pagan culture in Bible days did, our society has fallen for Satan's brazen lies. Homosexuality, extramarital affairs, Internet pornography, and emotional promiscuity are Satan's blatant tactics to catch us in his web of shame and captivity. As women, we are precious to the Lord, so please hear me out. If this is an area where you are weak, please know that you don't have to give in to the culture around you. If you are caught in this web of sexual temptation, you can be set free! I have precious friends, even relatives, who could sit down with you today and share with you how Jesus set them free from these particular yokes of bondage. Jesus Christ can fill every empty place in your heart that you are now trying to fill with sexual strongholds. You may justify your actions by saying cute quips like, "Sharon, I only go window shopping. I don't buy." That's a terrible deception. When we give in just a little, Satan turns up the heat.

Our lives are to be different from those living apart from Christ so that others may see Jesus in us. Paul warned, "Keep yourself pure" (1 Tim. 5:22) and minced no words toward Timothy when he instructed him to treat women "with absolute purity" (1 Tim. 5:2). Without reservation the Bible is totally against the popular trends of the day—living unmarried with a partner and having sex outside of the marriage bond is absolutely unacceptable according to biblical standards.

It is hard to pick up a women's magazine without reading of the tolerance or even the encouragement of sexual acts of women with men, women with women, incest, adultery, even in some cases bestiality. The headline I saw not too long ago, "Women are Handling the Affair Thing Just Fine," is absolutely not true.

I wish those who wrote that headline could sit with one woman who came to me after a recent women's conference. She had caught her husband in a sexual act with another woman and later learned that there had been many others. In addition, she learned that he also had been having an illicit relationship with their own daughter for years. How tragic! She was *not* handling the affair thing just fine. Believe me, this woman's heart was breaking.

The great enemy of every believer, Satan himself, spends much of his time devising schemes and ploys to trap and tempt spouses in this area. There is no doubt that he wants your marriage to fail. Bite by pernicious bite, he chomps away at what you know is true and pure.

He often lies to us, telling us that "the grass is greener on the other side." He wants you to believe that "pornography is a good sex educator and might make me a better lover." That's the statement one woman I'll call Jenny recently expressed to me. "We don't make love, we just have sex. My husband thinks the pornography will help me be a better partner. I hate what he's putting into our VCR."

Read with me what one author writes concerning this. "Pornography portrays an endless round of thrilling sexual escapades with an endless bevy of breathless, hot-blooded babes. And the not-so-subtle message is that these babes are more breathless and more hot-blooded if you're not married to them. But, an interesting thing happens when the playboy philosophy meets real life—it destroys sexual satisfaction."[18]

When pornography enters the home, a time bomb begins ticking. It will eventually explode with the destruction of an atomic bomb. Porn creates perversions, encourages multiple partners, encourages rape, increases the likelihood of extramarital affairs, produces incredible guilt and dissatisfaction with a spouse. It is a lie to believe that it will build greater intimacy.

None of us can afford to let our guards down. It I let loose a can of termites in your house and you were unaware—well, put it this way, it wouldn't take long before you would be aware! Your house would begin crumbling and weakening to the point that you would know that there were termites. Sadly, you probably wouldn't see the harm until it was too late—until the foundation crumbled. "For though we live in the world, we do not wage war as the world does" (2 Cor. 10:3).

I would encourage every Christian woman to read the book published by Focus on the Family entitled *An Affair of the Mind*.[19] This is a book that honestly and boldly confronts the pornography issues facing our families today. Laurie Hall learned of her husband's secret addiction to pornography after more than eighteen years of marriage. Through her rich faith grounded firmly in Christ and much research she found a way to reach out to her husband and they slowly began to rebuild their marriage. The book is compelling and to the point. Read it to open your eyes to truth or to give to a friend who may be in desperate need. Beverly LaHaye, chairman of the Concerned Women for America, says, "Read this book and you will never be the same." I whole-heartedly agree. No one can stay neutral on this deplorable subject after reading Laurie's story.

The issue that I am addressing is Satan's damaging dart in the area of his deceit. His lies tell you to let your guard down. His lies tell you to experiment. His lies tell you that R-rated movies aren't that bad. You see, the devil has no new tricks—he works the same old way he worked in the garden long ago. His ultimate goal is to make you and me think that it's okay to call the shots ourselves, to make up our own set of rules.

God has definitely given a woman a sexual beauty, feminine charm, and the ability to give physical pleasure to her husband. When used as God designed in the marriage relationship, sex is beautifully fulfilling. It works well the way God planned it to. A woman's sexual beauty is to be restrictive and exclusively for her husband. In modern days we have learned that it is not always the man who is unfaithful. How many homes are broken because of women who are unfaithful, women who fall into Satan's trap of believing, "It's all right. One little affair won't hurt." Ladies, God will not hold us guiltless! Before making a tragic mistake think of the consequences of just one such event. Think of the consequences to your reputation, your husband's reputation, the ridicule and pain your children will have to endure. The fleeting minutes of fun and flirtation are not worth the horrible days and perhaps even years of pain endured not just by you, but by those who are close to you. There is a day of reckoning. The consequences are great. Consider:

Emotional losses—Guilt, shattered marriages, depression, anxiety, lies

Spiritual losses—Loss of fellowship with God, deflated testimony (1 Cor. 6:18–20; Rom. 13:13–14)

Physical losses—Illegitimate pregnancies or births, sexually transmitted diseases

Sitting not too long ago beside a beautiful young woman, I noticed her shoulders began to shake; tears flow down her face. "I'm so scared," she began, "I know I need to make that phone call to end an affair with a married man, but I'm so afraid I can't do it." There was so much involved in mending four hurting lives. I asked God silently to help me not to come across as "holier than thou" and as we talked I did not press for many details. I just started out with Scripture—God's Word said it all. She made a determined decision to break off the relationship and made the call immediately. It was not easy. The marriage is mending and help is being received.

Infidelity is a devastation beyond repair for many couples. Don't become part of the statistics, I beg you. And don't play with fire. Trust me, every time, you will get burned. There are provoking, honest questions I ask myself often especially since my ministry involves travel without my husband at times. I may be naive, but I'm not dumb. You may want to ask yourself some of these questions to evaluate your behavior:

Do I behave and dress discreetly and properly around men?

Do I "put to death" (Col. 3:5–8) sinful, lustful, evil desires and greed?

Do I enhance my intimate relationship with my husband?

Do I avoid creating temptations and problems for other men?

Do I avoid establishing improper relationships with other men?

Let's use our heads! Learn to set limits. Sometimes we set up opportunities where it is too easy for Satan to step in with temptations at work, neighboring, even doing the Lord's work closely with men. We are not to give the devil a foothold (Eph. 4:27). Draw appropriate boundaries in your relationships.

I must add this important word. If you have already fallen into sexual sin, or know you are very vulnerable right now, run to the Lord. God offers deliverance and forgiveness. God loves and longs to forgive you. As with this or any other sin, He deals with it through His redemptive love.

One of my dearest friends in the world struggled for several years as a woman in the corporate world. She was exposed to sexual temptations often, as are many others. After a time of counsel and prayer together, she and I set up some strong limits for the specific conditions she would follow in business. I've listed some of those guidelines. You might want to impose some of the following upon yourself:

__I will not meet for lunch alone with men.

__I will include the names of both the husband and wife on letters or cards.

__During fellowship times, I will not give special attention to men.

__I will not listen to or give advice on personal issues with men (especially marital problems).

__Even if it costs me my job, I will avoid situations that set me up for temptation or could be misread by others and destroy my testimony for Christ.

God can use a clean vessel. "Do you not know that the wicked will not inherit the kingdom of God? Do not be deceived: Neither the sexually immoral nor idolaters nor adulterers nor male prostitutes nor homosexual offenders … will inherit the kingdom of God. And that is what some of you were …" (1 Cor. 6:9–11). It doesn't matter who you are, or what you've done, or where you came from—you can be a GIFT. It's not too late.

Dirty Dozen Dart #7—Disrespectful Wives

I like "The Andy Griffith Show" reruns on television. The other day one made me laugh out loud. It went something like this:

Andy asked his son, Opie, "Where'd you get that dog?"

"He followed me all the way home," was Opie's reply.

"What's that rope around his neck?"

"Oh, that was to make sure he followed me."

I suppose you knew we'd get to the "S" word sooner or later. Do we wives relate to "a rope around our neck" just like Opie had tied to his dog? We'll submit, we'll follow, but only if there's a rope.

There's no denying it—this is a major dart Satan throws at women today. Don't shy away, please. If you're not married, please don't skip over this section; you never know when you may need to recall its encouragement. Half of all marriages end in divorce. I contend that the misinterpretation and misunderstanding of submission is a major factor.

Perhaps you are like me and had such high hopes for marriage and expected your husband to make you happy forever. I had lofty visions of my being "Queen for a Day" every day! Isn't that marriage? *Duh!* Pretty unreasonable, huh? I was only inviting disillusionment and depression.

Only the Lord can bring about a happy marriage between two imperfect people. I learned that one the first month of marriage—I'm pretty quick, you know. I also learned during the first month of marriage that harping on failures to perform as promised only made me unattractive and unappealing to Rob. Well intended as I may have been, unwittingly I was quickly turning into the very thing I never wanted to be—a nag. If I was going to be a GIFT in my home, I needed to start being a present that Rob would want to receive.

Someone has said, "God will not use anyone greatly until He has crushed them mightily."

I hoped I'd be the exception. I was not.

It took a lot of refining and turning up the fire in this area for me to learn submission. (Some days I think I'm still in "SUBMISSION 101.") For thirty years God has kept His hand on the thermostat and turned up the heat! I really do love Rob; when you truly love someone, you want to love God's way. Scripture teaches that as the church submits to Christ, so also are we wives to submit to our husbands "in everything" (Eph. 5:24). God's way is to be a model of Christlikeness for your husband—it's a model of respect and honor.

Control is at the root of this submission subject. Satan will be sure to put roadblocks in the way to make wives not want to "be under or please the other person." But when we do, we demonstrate the very nature of Christ: "Who, being in very nature God, did not consider equality with God something to be grasped, but made himself nothing, taking the very nature of a servant (Phil. 2:6–7).

Christian marriages come in all shapes and sizes—all fall short of the perfect ideal in some way or another. Sometimes we treat submission as though it were the company china. It's just something to be brought out on occasion or for show in front of company. On a day-to-day basis mutual giving and "serving one another in love" is the God-given plea. Remember earlier in the book we filled in our names in the 1 Corinthians 13 spaces? Just as we need all those verbs in our actions towards our mates, we need the nouns of Galatians 5:22: love, joy, peace, patience, kindness, goodness, faithfulness, gentleness and self-control.

We do well to ask ourselves as wives these questions often:

Am I being immature?

Am I petty?

Do I constantly want my own way?

Will this matter tomorrow ... a year from now?

Am I selfish, impatient, intolerant?

Am I easily "irked"?

Am I jealous?

The Reverend Billy Graham says, "Marriage is a uniting of three persons—a man, a woman, and God! That is what makes marriage holy. Faith in Christ is the most important of all principles in the building of a happy marriage and a happy home."[20]

That doesn't sound like a rope has to be tied around our necks to get us to please and cooperate with our husband. Marriage was never intended to be a reform school or a place where we could correct every problem our husband has until he is whipped into shape. I've heard it said that there are four phrases that help in this matter:

They are: "I'm sorry." "I love you." "I was wrong." "Please forgive me."

What a gracious gift we give our children when they hear us say those phrases to our husbands. Search the Scriptures for passages on marriage. Good places to start would be:

> 1 Peter 3:7
> Ephesians 5:21–22
> 2 Corinthians 6:14–15
> Proverbs 24:3–4
> 2 Corinthians 7:39

Make the decision to love your husband—that's the plea in Ephesians. Not every day is going to be that easy, but it will always be blessed.

"Greater love has no one than this, that one lay down his life for his friends" (John 15:13). That certainly includes husbands!

Dirty Dozen Dart #8—Abortion

Yes, the devil aims this dart straight toward Christian women. You may be like a young teen girl who sincerely said to me "I didn't know it was a real baby." There are terrific resources from Focus on the Family available with the truth about abortion (including a great video that every teenage boy and girl alike should see). The American Tract Society in Garland, Texas, offers a small booklet called *The Sanctity of Human Life* with great verses supporting the biblical stand against abortion. The Bible has much to say about the life that God gives. This booklet states, "God fashions not only our lives as we live them day by day, but He was also planning our lives before we ever came on the scene."[21] God created life and a fetus is life.

David wrote thousands of years ago:

For you created my inmost being;
> You knit me together in my mother's womb.
I praise you because I am fearfully and wonderfully
>> made;
> your works are wonderful,
> I know that full well.
My frame was not hidden from you
> when I was made in the secret place.
When I was woven together in the depths of the earth,
> your eyes saw my unformed body.
All the days ordained for me were written in your book
> before one of them came to be.
(Ps. 139:13–16)

What value God places on human life! The embryo grow-ing inside the mother's body is more than just a part of her—it is another life! Job 12:10 says, "In his hand is the life of every creature and the breath of all mankind." "You shall not murder," Deuteronomy 5:17 clearly says.

If someone you know, or you, precious one, admits to the wrongness of abortion, please know that I am not here to lay guilt at your feet. Not for a minute—there is probably guilt enough for two lifetimes in your heart already. Taking the life of an unborn child will turn bad dreams into night-mares. Please ask God to bring good from the experience. He can! I've met young women who have suffered for a long time and God has worked all things for good. I've seen women put their arms around a young girl in love, accept-ance, and restoration—because they understand like only someone who's been there can.

"Neither do I condemn you," are Jesus' own words in John 8:11. "Go now and leave your life of sin."

Forgiveness is immediate, but a sense of acceptance and restoration can only come in time through a relationship with God. If you know someone considering an abortion, ask her to consider placing the precious little one for adoption. There are many Christian couples looking for a child to adopt to love and give a good home. Many organizations can help.

Psalm 32 is a psalm of joy for God's forgiveness: "Then I acknowledged my sin to you and did not cover up my iniq-uity. I said, 'I will confess my transgressions to the LORD'—and you forgave the guilt of my sin" (Ps. 32:5).

A Light for Your Path

The Word of God is transforming truth.

Don't continue to walk the roads marked "Shame." Be willing to turn and walk away from the intersection of impurity. On each of its four corners are signposts marked "Addictions," "Sexual Impurity," "Disrespectful Wives," and "Abortion." Don't go there anymore! Choose the higher ground, the path lit with Scripture, filled with road signs marked "Hope," paved with streets of neverending forgiveness and love. This route leads straight into the arms of Jesus. Let Him embrace you, comfort you, and heal you. We all must decide whether we will walk life's journey running toward God or fleeing away from Him. There is no in-between. Choose God. Draw near to Him and He will draw near to you. God is a loving God who will forgive and heal the hurts of His people. He'll trade your ashes for a crown of splendor and beauty.

Join me as we journey on, fellow traveler; we have one last chapter to go together. As we journey on just a little further, I pray your jaunt is wild and wonderful, whole and holy so that others will want to know how to join you. The next chapter will explain how that can happen.

PASSION

∞

A GIFTed woman inspires others to pursue their PASSION for Jesus Christ.

"The secret things belong to the LORD our God." Deuteronomy 29:29

Are you ready for one last secret? It's a biggie—it's the principal umbrella that spreads over everything else and makes all the other secrets possible.

First, a question for you. Let's be sincerely honest here. Who holds the remote control to the television in your house more often—you or your husband? I've asked that question at conferences to hundreds of women; the overwhelming answer is always the same. The vast majority of hands raise quickly when I ask, "Your husband?" Very few, I repeat, ver-rrrrry few are lifted when I ask, "How many of you, wives?" Generally there's a gaggle of giggling that follows, but secretly we all know deep down that we wish we could have answered differently. We wish we were in control. We *like* to be in control.

I know I do. Sometimes I race to grab the remote before Rob can sit down. I like the feeling of that remote control in the palm of my hand. It is the powerful feeling of control and I'm sad to say, I like it a lot—with the remote or with my life.

Ladies, "Man Your Battle Stations"

I didn't write this book to make you mad, or to make you feel like a failure, or to put you and me on a big guilt trip. The sole purpose of this book is to inspire and encourage each one of us to have an eternal influence on others in life-changing ways. Perhaps it all comes down to this last secret—Passion. In today's world we are in desperate need for women to be passionate about their Christian convictions and about living them out before others. Each of us has our unique "cross to bear"—a battle we're facing. Life is full of subtle, unsuspected, hidden skirmishes. I know my battles are far greater than I alone can conquer. The only way we're going to win in battle is to be exceedingly impassioned about our Captain and let Him be in control.

Let's stay honest here, sisters. Every morning you and I step into a new day of life—and a new battle for control. I'm finding out that my desire for control is a bad thing. A very bad thing. How perceptive is the woman who understands that she must have help in this area. Every warrior in the Bible who prevailed had those who helped him along the way. Without assistance, the chance of injury was greater and the likelihood of victory less. All the kings and great warriors of Scripture had armor bearers. The purpose of these armor bearers was to assist the soldier in battle by lightening his load. This enabled the soldier to be alert for the battle. There is strength in numbers.

In the same way, encouraging others to come along beside us to hold our arms up in battle is critical to ensure that we are protected from the enemy. We mutually need each other. As author and physician Elizabeth Kubler-Ross so aptly puts it: "The most beautiful people we have known are those who have known defeat, known suffering, known struggle, known loss, and have found their way out of the depths. These persons have an appreciation, a sensitivity, and an understanding of life that fills them with compassion, gentleness, and a deep loving concern. Beautiful people do not just happen."[22]

It is time to give up this "I can do-it-all, all-the-time, all-by-myself" mentality. "By self!" my Missy would demand when she was a two year old. Then she would proceed to throw a tantrum to further emphasize her point. Have you ever tried to pick up a two year old who has thrown herself down on the floor? You can't; the child renders you helpless. The only thing you can do is just walk away until the child is ready to cooperate.

Sometimes we are as unattractive as a squalling fit-throwing two year old. Even at thirty-, forty-, or fifty-something, we're still stomping our feet with unwavering belligerence, demanding to control things "By self!"

It's not very attractive. It often causes everyone to just

want to get away from us. No wonder we're losing the battles! It's time to challenge our hearts with these remaining darts in our provoking list of the Dirty Dozen. This issue of control is at the core of each. Ask yourself as you read, who is really in control of your heart in this out-of-control world? Even if the old devil has your life in chaos today, take hope. Let's not lose the war by refusing help from our Helper by erroneously pushing Him away with a proud, self-sufficient heart. I like this acrostic someone recently handed me for the word chaos:

Christ Has All Our Solutions.

That pretty much sums up this issue of control. Whatever, yes, *for whatever*—Jesus Christ has the answer if you will give Him the control. I'm not saying it is easy. Just like that old cliché, "Let go and let God." That is not easy. We like to hang on particularly tight to what (and whom) we treasure. I'm elated that you have joined me in my desire to influence others in profoundly meaningful ways. As you read through the remaining list that follows, make a definite, audible consecration of yourself in that area to God. Remember: What it is that has given you compassion? Where will you find your passion?

DIRTY DOZEN DART #9 — BUSYNESS

Are you a busy woman? Most women answer a resounding "Yes, I'm busy! Too busy!"

Today's helter-skelter world is a lot like the clowns we have seen spinning many plates in a circus. We get one plate spinning, then two, then three—by this time the first plate is wobbling—run over and give it a spin. You get the picture.

Have you ever wished for a thirty-hour day? If you are a living, breathing woman in the twenty-first century, you are going to be a busy person. Most of your time, like mine, is either spent going somewhere or returning from somewhere or planning where you need to go next. On and on our days go. Surely a few extra hours would relieve the pressure we live under, right? Delays and detours cramp our style because they deny us what we *just must get done!* For certain, nothing gets me in a major snit faster than when my plans don't go as I planned.

But would a thirty-hour day really solve the problem? Or would we just use the time to become even busier? It is not God who loads us with busyness until we break, have ulcers, nervous breakdowns, or heart attacks.

The following was a printed handout at a women's retreat where I was to speak. I admit my fear of speaking on the topic "Giving My Best" increased after reading what I share with you to follow. It became the catalyst for a life-change in my life.

> Satan called a world-wide convention. In his opening address to his evil angels, he said, "We can't keep the Christians from going to church. We can't keep them from reading their Bibles and knowing the truth. We can't even keep them from forming an intimate, abiding relationship with Jesus Christ. If they gain that connection with Jesus, our power over them is broken. So let them go to church, let them have their conservative lifestyles, but steal their time, so

they can't gain that experience in Jesus Christ. This is what I want you to do, angels. Distract them from gaining hold of their Savior and maintaining that vital connection throughout their day!"

"How shall we do this?" shouted his angels. "Keep them busy in the nonessentials of life and invent innumerable schemes to occupy their minds," he answered. "Tempt them to spend, spend, spend, and borrow, borrow, borrow. Persuade the wives to go to work for long hours and the husbands to work 6–7 days a week, 10–12 hours a day, so they can afford their lifestyles. Keep them from spending time with their children. As their family fragments, soon, their home will offer no escape from the pressures of work.

"Over-stimulate their minds so that they cannot hear that still, small voice. Entice them to play the radio or cassette player whenever they drive. And to keep the TV, VCR, CDs, and their PCs going constantly in their homes. And see to it that every store and restaurant in the world plays non-biblical music constantly. This will jam their minds and break that union with Christ.

"Fill the coffee table with magazines and newspapers. Pound their minds with the news twenty-four hours a day. Invade their driving moments with billboards. Flood their mailboxes with junk mail, sweepstakes, mail order catalogues, and every kind of newsletter and promotional offering free products, services, and false hopes. Even in their recreation be excessive. Have them return from their recreation exhausted, disquieted, and unprepared for the coming week.

"Don't let them go out in nature to reflect on God's wonders. Send them to amusement parks, sporting events, concerts, and movies instead. And when they meet for spiritual fellowship, involve them in gossip and small talk so that they leave with troubled consciences and unsettled emotion.

"Let them be involved in soul-winning. But crowd their lives with so many good causes they have no time to seek power from Christ. Soon they will be working in their own strength, sacrificing their health and family for the good of the cause."

It was quite a convention in the end. And the evil angels went eagerly to their assignments causing Christians everywhere to get busy, busy, busy and rush here and there.

Has the devil been successful in his scheme? You be the judge. How about this definition of busy: B—Being U—Under S—Satan's Y—Yoke.

How busy are you? It comes down to who or what controls your life. There are too many "uncontrollables" for you to manipulate circumstances by yourself. That's a battle Satan wants you to try to fight. Unconsciously, are you staying busy thinking you are "helping God out?" Perhaps you are pushing your agenda off on everybody else? Or watching TV hour after hour to escape from reality? "TV or not TV, that is the question." Rephrasing that famous Shakespearean line can help us all take inventory of the 86,400 seconds God gives us in a day. Not one person that I know of yet has ever said on their deathbed "I regret I didn't spend more time watching TV" or "Boy, I wished I'd spent more hours at the office."

I have three options:

I can WASTE my life.

I can SPEND my life.

I can INVEST my life.

Make a commitment to invest your life. Slow down. Prioritize. Bring your daily list before God—let Him number the items as to importance. Let Him make an alternative entry in your planner. Let your life inspire and influence others through your love, not impress them with your busyness.

What was the secret of Jesus' daily schedule? We find the answer in Mark 1:35: "Very early in the morning, while it was still dark, Jesus got up, left the house and went off to a solitary place, where he prayed." He prayed first thing to await His Father's instructions and to receive the strength to follow them. That was His secret way of being free from the tyranny of the urgent and accomplishing the important.

I know all too well what exhaustion and spiritual weariness feel like. I used to be too busy to sit still in a place of refuge. Like many, I used to admire the noise of busyness and a life lived at a frantic pace in our chaotic culture. But I don't want to go back to that wearying and unsatisfying lifestyle. Especially when its weariness shows not only in my heart, but also on my face!

Not long ago a friend whom I had not seen in almost a

year commented how relaxed and rested I looked. She immediately wanted to know what new face cream I'd discovered! I smiled to myself and tried to explain to my friend. She just didn't get it. She didn't even stay around long enough to hear the whole story. Hurriedly, on she ran, having more important things to do than to stand around listening to me talk about God making me to "lie down in green pastures." I'm glad you're taking the time to listen. When we spend time with God it does show on our faces. God's rest is the best beauty secret on the market!

God has given me a place of refuge from my busyness in a lovely deck that overlooks a most charming lake surrounded by trees. There's where I am learning to sit still. Just sit. Not doing anything—just sit. I listen to the little birds and watch them come and go from our feeder. I follow the gliding motions of the ducks on the lake and listen to the loud conversations of the frogs. Occasionally, a train whistles in the distance. Evenings take on a glow with the arrival of fireflies and candles flickering.

Here I rest in the presence of God. I *"be still and know that He is God."* I'm quiet enough to recognize His voice; not audibly, but unmistakably my heart hears Him. The thirst in my soul is quenched with sweet water from Himself, the Living Water.

In Stephen R. Covey's book *Seven Habits of Highly Effective People,* he tells a story that reflects the need for renewal and reawakening in our lives.

Suppose you were to come upon someone in the woods feverishly working to saw down a tree.

"What are you doing?" you ask.

"Can't you see?" comes the reply, "I'm sawing down this tree."

"You look exhausted!" you exclaim. "How long have you been at it?"

"Over five hours," he replies, "and I'm beat. This is hard work."

"Well, why don't you take a break for a few minutes and sharpen that saw?" you inquire. "I'm sure it would go a lot faster."

"I don't have time to sharpen the saw," the man says emphatically. "I'm too busy sawing."[23]

To sharpen the saw means renewing ourselves in all four aspects of our natures: physical, mental, social/emotional, and spiritual. To exercise in all these necessary dimensions, we must be pro-active. No one can do it for us or make it urgent for us. We must do it for ourselves.

> I waited patiently for the LORD;
>> he turned to me and heard my cry.
> He lifted me out of the slimy pit,
>> out of the mud and mire;
> He set my feet on a rock
>> and gave me a firm place to stand.
> He put a new song in my mouth,
>> a hymn of praise to our God.
> Many will see and fear
> and put their trust in the LORD.
> (Ps. 40:1–3)

DIRTY DOZEN DART #10 — DISHONESTY

Maybe this should have led the list of our Dirty Dozen. Never has there been a time when indifference and inconsistencies in regard to telling the truth existed more in the lives of Christian women. You might argue, "But there are varying degrees of honesty. After all, it's only a little white lie." To that I say—*too many Christians are trying to have one foot in the world and one foot in the kingdom of God*. When you straddle the fence, you're going to fall!

The Bible is so clear about the subject of trustworthiness in every aspect of our lives. "But now you must rid yourselves of all such things as these: anger, rage, malice, slander, and filthy language from your lips. Do not lie to each other ..." (Col. 3:8–9). Could it get any plainer? All through the Proverbs, as well, are countless verses regarding the praise of truth and the evils of dishonesty. Solomon, you were right! "He who finds a wife finds a good thing" (Prov. 18:22 NASB) ... especially when, "A wife of noble character who can find? She is worth far more than rubies. Her husband has full confidence in her and lacks nothing of value" (Prov. 31:10–11). Do your husband and family members put trust in you?

Trustworthy. Honest. Faithful. Those words depict a person who can be trusted to faithfully transact business and carry out honest dealings in life. Is that what others think of when they hear your name? Honest women are to be honored. When I have a friend who is dishonest, I don't trust her with precious people, possessions, or jobs. Honesty is a quality that I look for when assigning even small, seemingly insignificant jobs.

We've all known people who omit important details, misrepresent stories, and create confusion by telling half-truths. Do you trust those people with confidential information about yourself? Of course not. It is too big a risk. When credibility is lost, either in marriage or a job or in your personal testimony, it is hard to rebuild.

I understand the temptations in our society to fudge a little here and there. Be cautious! Don't fall for the lie of Satan that says, "it doesn't matter." Yes, it does! We can't afford to be too nit-picky about this—remember Sapphira? She was married to Ananias. Her name meant "beautiful," but her lack of integrity was not pretty at all. God used her to teach us all a lesson. Caught in a deliberate lie when questioned by Peter about the price of the sale of their land, Sapphira immediately fell down and died (Acts 5:1–11). This stunned the Jerusalem church, but it taught an important lesson. *God allows no dishonesty and deceit in His relationship with His people.*

Are we to make the same fatal mistake? God places a high value on the truth, and nothing but the truth. What about when the clerk gives me back too much change? Or, as in my case a few months ago, am I to go back and tell the department store that I bought the shoes that were actually the ones not in the ad for five dollars less? I didn't figure it out until I unpacked my bags at home. Doesn't it all even out? I'm sure there have been times when I didn't receive enough change back. Right?

Wrong! Wearily, I went all the way back up to the store and paid the five dollars. You know what? I'm so glad did. I didn't have to wrestle a troubled conscience—that made the bother worthwhile. Plus, I knew Jesus would have me do it. One of my friends protested, "But, it won't matter or hurt anyone if I sign my son's reading report. He did almost read twenty books." Her call. I was not going to tell her what to do, but I did share what I thought was the right thing to do. If it's not the whole truth, it's not the truth. Every time I stretch the truth, I'm eroding my character. Even if no one else gets hurt, I would be hurting myself.

Telling children to answer the phone and say we are not home or misrepresenting a homework assignment is teaching them that lying is okay. The world wants them to think that it is; God's Word says it is not. Emphatically. I recently found that there are over 200 references to being vigilant to the truth in the Bible.

Lying becomes such a habit for some women that it becomes similar to alcoholism. Even though they do not pick up the drink they are addicted to feeling "in the know" or superior. Lying becomes a way of life because they are frightened of abandonment in relationships.

"The LORD detests lying lips, but he delights in men who are truthful" (Prov. 12:22). And in this poignant list of things God hates, lying is second and a false witness is sixth: "There are six things the LORD hates, seven that are detestable to him: haughty eyes, a lying tongue, hands that shed innocent blood, a heart that devises wicked schemes, feet that are quick to rush into evil, a false witness who pours out lies and a man who stirs up dissension among brothers" (Prov. 6:16–19).

Only you can honestly answer the question, "Am I honest?" Would you be embarrassed if everyone knew your secret dealings, thoughts, words, and deeds? God knows. He looks on the heart, not the outward appearance. When you think you are fooling everyone, don't kid yourself. Dishonesty on the outside is a reflection of dishonesty on the inside. God sees and knows and someday we will all be accountable to Him.

My husband and I have little as far as material things of this life are concerned. Being in fulltime Christian service, we probably never will. But that certainly doesn't discourage or defeat us. We have much more than many and consider ourselves wealthy in the things of the Lord. One of those blessings is the gift of being able to sleep well at night, knowing that our consciences are clear of dishonesty and deception. That is bountiful wealth that money can't buy—a price far above rubies.

I'll never forget the time I stood in the little home of a pastor's wife in the Philippines and saw the humble dwelling where they lived. With a sincere thankful heart she "toured" me through the three rooms. They were of very modest means, but the woman beamed and her eyes glistened from within as she walked to a corner and said, "And this is our chair." That's right—just one in the whole house. I marveled at how her life exemplified honesty, integrity, and right up there at the top—thankfulness.

Anchor your integrity to the Word of God—that alone is what helps prevent us from yielding to the temptations of dishonesty. Maybe no one else is doing what's right, but you and I can. Regardless of what everyone else is doing, let's just do what's right! We can be honest. We can take a stand. We can be true. The majority is not always right. If the majority ruled, David would never have fought Goliath. He would have stayed in the fields with the sheep.

You and I must listen to God's heart—not everyone else's words. When faced with tough decisions; take heart—when we do what is right, God sees and God remembers.

DIRTY DOZEN DART #11 — CHILD ABUSE

Be very clear on this—God in no way approves of mistreatment of a child. Children are loved as cherished gifts from God. Abuse in any nature is reprehensible and I believe God hates it and is sad. We are raising children in a high-strung, neurotic, impatient, hurried time. And there's no reason to hurry—we're just rushing children more than any previous generation.

Proverbs 29:15: "The rod of correction imparts wisdom, but a child left to himself disgraces his mother." Discipline is to teach—not to punish. Be sure to be tender, sensitive, and always loving in your approach to a child. Cruel, harsh treatment echoes in a little one's mind for a long, long, time. I remember as an eight-year-old little girl being criticized so sharply in my second grade class that I thought I would die on the spot.

I was enjoying an art project and just cutting and pasting away. That's when my teacher shouted in a thunderous voice, "That is *not* the way to cut—you don't know how to cut on the lines!" Hovering right above me, she then yanked my construction paper out of my hand and, as if the shouting weren't bad enough, she held up my poor cutting as an example for the whole class to see how not to cut.

Her words and humiliation hurt deeply. I was crying by the time she demanded that I march to the front of the classroom and throw my project into the trash can and start again. "It was so bad!" It was a cruel and degrading thing to do. I was only an eight-year-old child and the brand-new kid in school at that. I was not used to being screamed at.

The message that came across loud and clear as I took the long walk up to the trash can to throw away something I valued, was "You can't do anything right." My teacher probably did not intend to, but she stripped me of all my self-esteem in that class that day. My spirit was crushed. I remember not enjoying much of the rest of the school year and doing every project in fear of embarrassment.

If you have anger problems, there may be underlying unresolved hurts from your childhood to be dealt with. Dr. James Dobson's books, *Hide or Seek* and *Dare To Discipline*, are wonderful resources that every mother needs. His teaching on spanking and on reinforcing good, proper behavior is absolutely the best.

God is not pleased when we take out our "low boiling point" on a child. Speak in love, not accusation or judgment. We adults are to look out for a child's highest welfare. When you know someone who is abusing a child, help the person understand the harm that comes when we mistreat "the least of these." Let them know that physical abuse is against the law and they can be severely punished for it. With God's help, control is possible. Child abuse is one family secret that needs counseling and, often, long-term help getting to deep-rooted problems.

Proverbs 22:6 says we are to "train a child." I do believe children get punished many times because they simply are children. They're going to make childish mistakes and we adults need to realize that. Accidents do happen. Just about the time I got in a snit about one of my girls spilling the milk, you guessed it! I would spill my milk!

"Let the little children come to me" (Matt. 19:14).

"And we urge you, brothers, warn those who are idle, encourage the timid, help the weak, be patient with everyone" (1 Thess. 5:14).

DIRTY DOZEN DART #12 — WORRY

Do you ever have situations in your life where you wonder if everything will turn out all right? I remember the time when I trusted Jesus Christ as my Savior as an eight year old. I felt so clean; so happy; I remember thinking to myself, "Now that I'm saved, I won't have problems anymore, or be afraid, or do bad things." Each of us can probably identify with the relief and joy of becoming a brand-new child in the faith. However, it wasn't too long until I began to see that I still sinned, still had worries, and still had other problems. I was one disappointed little girl. I also was one fearful, worried little girl. I worried much about the lack of control over my life and was preoccupied with the worry and fears of abandonment. Even as a youngster, worry was the enemy's tool to paralyze me.

Not a lot changed in this area as I grew into adulthood. Bless my heart, I still worried. I worried about some of the same issues I'd held onto since I was little. But God honors a heart that longs to change. I wanted change! I so wanted to conquer this worry thing. When we make room in our hearts for God to do what He longs to do, a wonderful thing happens—we give God freedom to work things out *His way, not ours.* Worry dissolves and innermost feelings of security begin to emerge. God has a chance to replace and erase our worry and fill us with trust. That's how generous God was with me—so gracious. The more pressures I felt, the more He pressed me to His heart.

Day by day, I was encouraged in my quiet time to keep my mind centered on Jesus Christ and what He tells us to think upon in Philippians 4. I was promised that "perfect peace" would be the result. I was not disappointed.

Worry does not change anything; only the Word can. Worry only draws our focus away from God instead of toward God. Only when we yield whatever it is we're worried about to God can we find peace. In essence we are saying, "God, I think about the situation I'm worried about today; and this is how I feel about it. I don't have an answer. I don't see you in all this, but somehow, some way, I know You will work this all out." The Lord came to set us free! By bringing our specific worries to the Lord and asking for His help, we realize we can begin to trust Him.

Through Christ we can claim our ultimate gift of worry-free living and influence others to do the same. I am discovering that the battle is won or lost in my mind. Setting my mind on

Christ is the process involved in putting on our new self, then being renewed in the knowledge of Him (see Eph. 4:23–24).

Doing the "What If" thing is my big worry struggle. *What if* I can't get a project done? *What if* I have offended someone? *What if* I am unable to properly handle a situation? I debate, disbelieve, doubt, and analyze. All too often I meet women who do the same. They "what if?" But many women I speak with about this subject are worried and have no idea about what. They say they are "just worried." A beautiful little lady expressed at a retreat her worry by exclaiming, "I worry about everything and everybody. Then I worry because I'm so worried."

God's antidote to worry for her and all of us is actually a simple formula:

prayer + supplication + thanksgiving = peace

This is a peace that "transcends all understanding" and "will guard your hearts and your minds" (Phil. 4:7). Worry dissipates when we acknowledge our dependence on God and submit to His leadership.

I know all too well how frightening it is to live a prisoner in my own thoughts. Stress took its toll and robbed me of the abundant life that Jesus talks about for far too long. I wasted so much energy on the "What Ifs," but now I'm glad I've had to deal with severe anxiety—it has forced me to form some "heal thyself" thinking patterns, to think upon these things: whatever is true, noble, right, pure, lovely, and admirable (Phil. 4:8).

The apostle Paul says we render sin's power ineffective when we consider or reckon ourselves dead to the impulses and pull of our sin nature. That turns off the power of our sin nature! Instead we consider ourselves alive and responsive to God in Christ Jesus!

God's peace is always available—but we must choose it. That's the key part of the secret here. We can choose to stand shriveling in the scorching, hot sun of worry and be burned, parched, and dry—or choose to move over into the cool, comforting shade of God's peace. It takes some time to overcome an ingrained habit of worry. But in time, trust and confidence are built, so hang in there. Don't quit and give up—you will gain more strength in Him. Trusting God is one of those areas in which we have to get experience for ourselves. It doesn't come easily for many people. On the Christian journey, one of the main reasons for getting off the road is worrying and not trusting. Worry does nothing to change your situation, but placing the problem in the hands of Jesus can. That changes everything.

A Prayer for Combating Worry

Father God, help me today not to worry. I choose to keep my mind on You and on Your Word, not on my situation. I cast all my cares upon You, for I know that You deeply care for me. I trust in You to take care of me today like You take care of the birds of the air and the lilies in the field. I know You have a good plan for my life. I hold on to that promise. Fulfill that plan in me today. In Jesus' name, amen.

Conclusion

The Remote—My New Best Friend

After, shall we say, an altercation (I'm trying to find a nicer way of saying *big argument!*) over the remote control one evening with Rob while selecting TV channels, I exited the family room in quite a snit. Well, okay, I left in more like a fury. I'd forgotten it was Monday night. Monday night during football season. Monday night at our house means football. Only football. After slamming the remote down with a loud whack, I remember saying something like, "There. It's yours. You can be in control." I promptly (and loudly) exited to the back porch.

It took awhile to see what had just gone on in there. It was really that control issue again. I remember praying aloud in the swing on our deck for the one thing I wanted most. "Lord, I submit. The passion of my life is to know Your perfect will for my life and to live it out." That was it! I felt entirely free. The load of control was lifted. I didn't have to straighten out messes or solve problems or figure out where the rest of my life was going. Praise God, I didn't have to be in control.

Neither do you.

God will be—if we just let Him. After all, He is the blessed Controller. In the same way that I let go of the remote and laid it down, I prayed that God would help me to take my hands off allowing Him to control my life. Later that evening, I walked back into the family room and apologized to Rob for my ugliness. It's been eleven months now, almost a year since that day. I cannot begin to tell you of the peace that I have in my heart. The burden of my having to straighten everything out is lifted. The answer seemed to come right out of heaven itself—lay down the control. Have I had to pray that same prayer since? Oh yes, emphatically, yes!

Just this morning, walking past our sofa table, I caught sight of that same remote control. It serves as a reminder to surrender control. What used to look like a lot of fun to have in the palm of my hand, really isn't that appealing at all now.

Gripping it only reminds me of how much I need to let it go.

What looks like the worst disappointment or disaster in your life right now may very well turn out to be the very springboard of a mighty influence you will have on others' lives. It's what you were created for. Let God choose the gift-wrap and allow Him to wrap you in His love the way He sees fit. Is it any wonder that God shares His secrets with us and asks us to share them with others?

Don't expect miracles overnight. Remember, the

Christian life is lived by being "crucified with Christ" (Gal. 2:20). Living is actually about dying: dying to self; letting God be in charge instead of ourselves. We are to reckon ourselves dead indeed to sin—alive to Christ. Alive to share His secrets! Remember the words Jesus spoke to Mary Magdalene in John 20:17? He asked her to go and tell his disciples that she had seen him. Jesus didn't require her to be an articulate speaker or memorize the entire Old Testament. He simply asked her to tell what she'd seen and heard—that He was alive!

Everything of genuine worth takes time and practice. These twelve spiritual secrets do work when made a real part of your life and applied over a period of time—with persistence. Don't give up (or panic) when you fail. I do; we all do. As you begin to apply these principles, you're going to blow it frequently. I pray you are better equipped to go out today and share Jesus Christ, the best gift of all.

Begin each day with a simple prayer: "Lord, Your will be done. I'm going to take my hands off the control and let You take over. Make me a gracious GIFTed woman—a *Godly Influencer For Today*. Help me to touch my world for eternity." Remember: He's the Gift, you are the package—wrap yourself in His love and picture a bow on the top of your head. I often do just that. No, I don't tie a Shirley Temple bow around my ringlets, but I wear an array of ribbon silver or gold pins at my lapel that often become a tool of witnessing for Christ. They are a great reminder to me of what I'm to be about as I get dressed and go out to face the day. How I pray these secrets God has impressed upon my heart will continue to whisper in your ears for a long, long time. I trust they have influenced your life.

Author and speaker Carol Kent says it best when she says, "Becoming a woman of influence is costly, risky, and time-consuming, but there can be no greater joy than knowing you have obediently begun to impact others by shaping hearts to the image of Jesus Christ."[24]

Keep your eyes on the gracious Giver and be a godly influence to someone today. God wants to come to the people in your life through you. What an opportunity for you to minister to the needs of your family, friends, and even strangers at the checkout counter where you shop. You never know how much of a gift you can be until you let God make you that GIFT. The happiest people I know are the ones who have said, "I let go and let God control my life. Now, I yield the very battle I've been losing. By faith, I will go out and make a difference in my world!" This may come as a big shock to you (it was to me) but, when something unfortunate is happening to us, it's actually an answer to a prayer we've prayed of submission.

"You can be sure that the Lord will be with you and help you successfully stand against whatever opposes you. When you walk with Him in the battle, you're never alone."[25] You see, winning the battle begins with surrender. It still astounds me that when we let God win our battles, He gives us a ministry of influence we never set out to have—to those who are overwhelmed with the same battles we used to have. As you travel down the road of life, put into practice the commands of Psalm 91:1–2. Dwell in the secret place of the Most High under the shadow of the Almighty, leaning on Him, making Him your refuge and fortress.

Join me in a prayer that captures the meaning of each of the GIFTed secrets: "Father, it is my heart's hunger and desire to abandon my whole self to You and Your will. I am amazed and thrilled that someone as wonderful as You could love me and want my love in return. I am committed to being a woman and a godly influence, changing my world for eternity. Do what You must to open and remodel my heart so I can know the deepest joy in and be just like Jesus in:

Power

Purpose

Precious Acceptance

Prayer

Praise

Patience

Perseverance

Perspective

Privilege

Past Your Past

Purity

Passion

Lord, that is my highest goal, my delight for time and eternity. I pray that day by day I'll discover more fully how perfect your intensely personal, never-ending love is. To You be the glory and honor—forever and forever. Amen."

Rest assured; when God starts His work in your life, He *will* complete it. That's His promise (see Phil. 1:6). He knows just where you need to go and just what you are going to do for Christ when you get there. Don't stop God's work until He is finished. Let Him remodel your heart. Don't just allow Him to add a picture or two on the wall, but let Him tear down some walls. Walls of anger can be demolished and your shaky foundation restored. You can trust Jesus. He sees your future. He'll be right there beside you wiping your tears in times of sorrow and cheering you on during times of triumph.

Now, you know the secrets. Secrets to be just like Jesus. This is the GIFTed woman that you, yes *you*, can become—Christ-centered, Christ-controlled. Let God do amazing things with your life. Leave this world better than you found it.

NOTES

Secret #2: PURPOSE

1 Facts drawn from articles in *Pop Star Magazine*: "A Tribute To Princess Diana," Volume 1, No. 7 (New York: Biograph Communications, 1997).

2 Al Jansen. *Choices for Graduates* (Grand Rapids: Baker Book House, 1988), 26.

3 James Dobson. *What Wives Wish Their Husbands Knew About Women* (Carol Stream, Ill.: Tyndale House Publishers, 1975).

Secret #3: PRECIOUS ACCEPTANCE

4 Henry Blackaby. *Experiencing God: Knowing and Doing the Will of God* (Nashville: LifeWay Press, 1990), 42.

5 Archibalt Hart. *Fifteen Principles for Achieving Happiness* (Waco: Word Publishing, 1988), 114.

6 Sandra D. Wilson. *Released from Shame* (Downer's Grove: InterVarsity Press, 1990), 115.

Secret #4: PRAYER

7 Becky Tirabassi. *Let Prayer Change Your Life* (Nashville: Thomas Nelson, 1992).

Secret #5: PRAISE

8 Sarah Ban Breathnach. *Simple Abundance: A Daybook of Comfort and Joy* (Boston: Warner Books, 1995).

9 Frank Minirth and Paul Meier. *Happiness Is a Choice: The Symptoms, Causes, and Cures of Depression* (Grand Rapids: Baker Book House, 1994).

Secret #6: PATIENCE

10 Billy Graham. *Christian Worker's Handbook* (Minneapolis: World Wide Publications, 1984), 187.

11 Carol Mayhall. *Help, Lord, My Whole Life Hurts* (Colorado Springs: NavPress, 1988), 42.

Secret #7: PERSEVERANCE

12 Beth Nimmo and Debra K. Klingsporn. *The Journals of Rachel Scott* (Nashville: Thomas Nelson, 2001), 4–5.

13 Misty Bernall. *She Said Yes* (Plough Publishing House, 1999).

14 Carmerin Courtney. "Higher Calling," *Today's Christian Woman*, (November-December 2002.

15 Lisa Beamer. *Let's Roll* (Carol Stream, Ill.: Tyndale House Publishers, 2002); and "Influencing a Nation, Influencing Her Family," *Today's Christian Woman*, September 2002.

Secret #9: PRIVILEGE

16 C. S. Lewis. *Reflections on the Psalms* (New York: Harcourt, Brace, Jovanovich, 1958), 90-91.

17 Kay Arthur. *Lord, I Want to Know You: A Devotional Study on the Names of God* (Colorado Springs: NavPress, 2000).

Secret #11: PURITY

18 Laurie Hall. *An Affair of the Mind* (Colorado Springs: Focus on the Family, 1996), 78.

19 Ibid.

20 Billy Graham. *The Christian Worker's Handbook* (Minneapolis: World Wide Publications, 1984).

21   *The Sanctity of Human Life,* available from American Tract Society, PO Box 462008, Garland, Texas 75046.

Secret #12: PASSION

22   Life Challenges; http://www.lifechallenges.org/create/quickquote.html (October 23, 2003).

23   Stephen R. Covey. *Seven Habits of Highly Effective People* (New York: Simon & Schuster, 1989), 287.

CONCLUSION

24   Carol Kent. *Becoming a Woman of Influence* (Colorado Springs: NavPress, 1999), 170.

25   Stormie Omartian. *Just Enough Light For the Step I'm On,* (Eugene, Oregon, Harvest House, 1999), 69.

YOUR LIFE JOURNEY

THE
G.I.F.T.ed
WOMAN

**A GUIDE FOR PERSONAL REFLECTION
OR GROUP DISCUSSION**

YOUR LIFE JOURNEY

∞

Are you gifted? You might shrug your shoulders and look away when someone talks about your giftedness. Life overwhelms you, and "gifted" is the last thing you feel.

You're not gifted because of your own talents. You're not gifted because of your own accomplishments. You're not gifted because of your own organizational skills. You're gifted because of what God does for you. And he wants to do plenty. Are you ready to tap into the giftedness that God has for you? That's what this book is all about—discovering the gifts that God gives women so that they can pass those gifts on to the people in their lives.

The GIFTed woman has a Godly Influence For Today. She touches the lives of children, husband, coworkers, neighbors, friends, volunteers at the PTA—strangers in the supermarket—because God has touched her. Every day, you as a woman have the opportunity to encourage and build up the people around you. But who encourages and builds up you? God's Spirit is within you, shaping you, forming you, prodding you, speaking to you. Are you listening?

This book helps you take time to reflect on the gifts God has for you to pass on to others around you. Each chapter looks at one aspect of spirituality and encourages you to pause in your private "rat race" for a few minutes to absorb some Scripture, stories, and personal reflections. Take one chapter at a time, soak it up, and make it personal.

How is God calling you? What is He making you into? Whose life is He preparing you to touch? Let Him make you ready for the days and years to come. Be a gift in the lives of the people you love.

SECRET #1: POWER

A GIFTed woman has access to God's power to do the impossible.

Many women feel powerless in some situations—or even in all situations. In what ways do you sometimes feel powerless? How does knowing that you have access to God's power help in these situations?

What is the difference between giving up and giving up to God? What areas of your life do you think God wants you to give up to Him rather than just "give up"?

When Sharon was ready to get out of the car and get out of her whole life, her husband, Rob, wouldn't give up on her. Who do you have in your life who won't give up on you? How does this person strengthen your weak faith?

Read the story of Elijah and the widow at Zarephath in 1 Kings 17:8–16. In what ways do you identify with this woman? What can you learn from Elijah's actions that might help in your difficult situations?

What situation in your life seems most impossible to you right now? Pray right now for God's power in that situation.

SECRET #2: PURPOSE

A GIFTED Woman purposes to live in the light of eternity.

A woman's day is filled with many roles, multiple tasks, and constant interruptions. Often most of the things that happen in a day seem to have no long-lasting point. How do you respond when you have a day like this?

Diana, Princess of Wales, had a fairy tale wedding—but her life was no fairy tale. What parts of your life have not turned out the way you hoped and dreamed? How do you think God has worked in those areas despite how they turned out?

Sharon says, "Getting our priorities right is the first step in living a life of purpose." What are your top five priorities? Do you think other people can tell what your priorities are by your everyday actions and words?

What do you hope that people will say about you on your eighty-fifth birthday?

What obstacles get the way of your having a time of personal retreat? Make a plan for getting past the obstacles for a day of hearing from the Lord about the purpose of your life. Make some notes about what you would like to do with a day of personal retreat.

Esther discovered the purpose God had for her life under difficult circumstances that she never expected. How has God used unexpected circumstances to reveal purposes He has for your life?

SECRET #3: PRECIOUS ACCEPTANCE

A GIFTed woman finds precious acceptance and value in Jesus Christ.

"I have loved you with an everlasting love; I have drawn you with loving-kindness" (Jeremiah 31:3). How do you personally respond to this verse?

What makes you feel precious and valued? How does God make you feel precious and valued?

In what ways was your earthly father a picture of the acceptance your heavenly father offers? In what ways did your earthly father blur the picture of your heavenly father?

Our misperceptions about God sometimes keep us from believing that we are precious to Him. Sometimes our earthly relationships set us up to believe we are not worthy of acceptance. How have these concepts been true in your life?

Sharon tells much of her own story, her own struggle to believe she is valuable to God and to others. What is your story? Can you identify relationships or experiences that are still getting in the way of believing how much God values you?

Read the Bible verses under "God's Facts" on page xxx. Which one of these verses strikes home for you the most? Why?

SECRET #3: PRAYER

A GIFTed woman cultivates the private practice of prayer.

Sharon tells the story of how God spoke to her through a message printed inside the cover of an egg carton—an unexpected message at an unexpected but ordinary moment. How does God speak to you through ordinary moments?

Read Luke 10:38–42. In what ways are you like Martha? In what ways are you like Mary? How would you like to change?

What are your personal habits of prayer? Where? How? When? How satisfied are you with your prayer habits? What would you like to change?

Many people find it difficult to focus on prayer for more than a few moments at a time. Using a prayer journal can be helpful. How do you think that writing out your prayers would help you?

Sharon says, "I am not naïve enough to assume that prayer is natural or easy for you." In what ways is prayer hard for you? What would it take for prayer to become natural in your life?

How do you think a richer prayer life would help you be a more godly influence in the people in your life?

SECRET #5: PRAISE

A GIFTed Woman wraps herself in a pleasant package of praise.

"If only …" How many times a day do you catch yourself saying "If only I had…." Does this attitude help you or hurt you?

How can you cultivate a thankful heart that expresses itself in praise?

Sharon says, "Sometimes we have to suffer great defeat to appreciate the little victories in life. Never forget that God is more interested in our character than our comfort." What experiences has God used to mold a character of praise in you?

"Contentment is not a natural quality for most people." How true is this statement of you? What is the relationship between contentment and praise in your life?

Sharon suggests that a heart of praise is a choice we make every day. What keeps you from choosing praise? What helps you to choose praise?

Complete this thought in five different ways: "Today I praise God for …"

SECRET #6: PATIENCE

A GIFTed woman is continually learning patience—waiting on God's timing, trusting that in time, God will make clear His glorious plan.

If you were teaching a class called Patience 101, what would you include in your lesson plans?

Why is waiting frustrating? What good has come from waiting in your own life?

What is the danger in seeking "quick fixes" that don't require patience?

Sharon suggests a number of reasons we get impatient (pages 119-121). Which of these is most true of you? On an index card, write the verse that Sharon suggests as an answer to this cause. Put it up somewhere where you will see it often.

Sharon tells several brief stories as examples of what we might give up in order to have God's best. What do you think God is calling you to give up in order to have His best for you?

What other biblical examples of patience can you think of, in addition to the ones the author suggests?

SECRET #8: PERSEVERANCE

A GIFTed woman recognizes that she cannot choose life's circumstances, but she can respond to each stage with strength, stamina, and a staying perseverance.

The author tells about her "portion," her life's cup—circumstances and experience that she has had to overcome. What is in your cup?

What does the secret of perseverance follow the secret of patience?

How do you respond when God doesn't answer prayers the way you wanted?

Sharon recounts the stories of a number of women who stood up for their beliefs in God and persevered through difficult times. What can you learn from these women that you can apply in your own life?

Paul's secret was his relationship with Christ. You can read about what he endured in 2 Corinthians 11:24–28. His answer to everything he endured is found in 2 Corinthians 12:9–10. How would you paraphrase this verse to make it personal for you?

Sharon challenges us to put our lives in God's hands and describes God's hands as full of majesty and power, outstretched, and compassionate. In what ways have you seen

God's hands majestic and powerful, outstretched, and compassionate in your life circumstances?

SECRET #8: PERSPECTIVES

A GIFTed woman intentionally involves and invests her life in future generations by passing on godly **perspectives to the** *younger women in her world.*

Read Titus 2:3–5,12. Write down three important thoughts you can take away from this passage.

What older women have been positive models for you? What perspectives on life have you gained from them?

What giftedness do you have to share with younger women in your life?

Reaching out to younger women is not easy for everyone. What keeps you from reaching out more? What scares you about reaching out? What brings you joy when you reach out to share godly perspectives?

Sharon says, "what younger women need is not someone with an impressive resume or someone who will help them 'find themselves.' No, they need a women who will help them find God." How can one woman help other women find God in practical ways?

What ideas can you add to Sharon's list for ways to reach out to a younger woman? Make your list personal.

If you could offer one piece of spiritual advice to a younger woman, what would it be?

SECRET #9: PRIVILEGE

A GIFTed woman fixes her focus heavenward through the privilege of worshiping Jesus Christ.

Sharon sees worship as a joyful privilege. In what ways is worship a joy for you?

"God longs for true worship to be the priority of our hearts." What keeps us from making worship a priority? How can you get past the obstacles to worship in your own life and heart?

Sharon suggests six characteristics of a worship experience: solitude, silence, sincerity, surrender, Scripture, and singing. Which one of these is hardest for you? Which one is most natural? Why do you think that is?

One way to worship is to reflect on the names of God that appear in Scripture. Some of these are listed on page 189. Which one of these is the most personal for you? How would focusing on this name affect your worship?

How would you summarize your own personal habit of worship? What would your like your personal habit of worship to be like? How can you move closer to that goal?

What three words would you use to describe the difference that worship can make in your spiritual life?

SECRET #10: PAST YOUR PAST

A GIFTed woman leaves the prisons of the past behind.

How would you summarize the difference between impressing and impacting others with godliness?

Sharon says that "forgiveness is a choice." What keeps you from choosing to forgive? What keeps you from receiving forgiveness?

What kinds of experiences push your anger button? How do you feel about the way you behave when you're angry? What experiences do you need to leave behind in order to get past your anger?

As she discusses a critical, judgmental spirit, Sharon suggests these three questions: Is this a wise thing to say? Is this an uplifting thing to say? Is this a true thing to say? If you stopped to ask these questions throughout your day, how would that affect what comes out of your mouth? How would it affect what goes through your mind?

We all feel depressed from time to time. Some of us suffer from true clinical depression. Why is it important to recognize the difference? What do you think is the relationship between anger and depression?

Sharon learned a valuable lesson from an ordinary flower in a mountain meadow. What ordinary items does God use to help you get past your painful past?

SECRET #11: PURITY

A GIFTed woman lives a life of purity based upon absolutes in God's Word.

Sharon talks about compulsions and addictions that so easily can take control of us. What do you find yourself doing on a continuing basis even though you really wish you didn't? What would it take to make you stop?

Our modern culture is saturated with sexual images. What specific challenges from our culture make sexual purity difficult?

Why is it so easy to "let down our guard" when it comes to sexual purity? In what ways have you struggled with sexual purity, whether you have acted on your thoughts or not?

What personal guidelines do you have for preserving

your sexual purity? If you are married, what precautions to you take to be sure you don't cross your own lines?

Sharon discusses disrepectfulness in the context of purity? How are purity and respectfulness for your spouse related in your own life?

One consequence of sexual impurity is unplanned pregnancy, which may lead to abortion. Even married women, however, may turn to abortion as a solution to whatever problem they face. How does thinking about the subject of purity based in God's Word affect how you feel about abortion?

Abortion carries many emotional and psychological consequences that women are not aware of when they choose abortion. If you know a woman who has had an abortion and now suffers regrets, what can you do to help her find God's forgiveness?

SECRET #12: PASSION

A GIFTed woman inspired others to pursue their passion for Jesus Christ.

Sharon says, "The sole purpose of this book is to inspire and encourage each one of us to have an eternal influence on others in life-changing ways." How has this book changed the way you think about influencing others?

On a scale of 1 to 10, how passionate are you about living out your Christian convictions? Be honest! How far away are you from the number you'd like to be able to say?

Many of us might say that busyness gets in the way of living out our passion. We just get overwhelmed with the mundane things we have to do each day. Sharon says we have three options: we can waste our lives, we can spend our lives, or we can invest our lives. What would you like to invest your life in?

What value do you put on the truth? Are you someone that others can trust because you handle the truth wisely?

How does worry keep you from pursuing your passion for Jesus Christ? Read Philippians 4:6–7. How do these verses help you put worry in perspective?

If you could do one thing differently in order to pursue your passion for Jesus Christ, what would it be?

CONCLUSION

Throughout the book, Sharon talks about journaling and writing prayers. Write a prayer in your own words asking God to help you be a GIFTed woman.

The Word at Work . . .

*W*hat would you do if you wanted to share God's love with children on the streets of your city? That's the dilemma David C. Cook faced in 1870s Chicago. His answer was to create literature that would capture children's hearts.

Out of those humble beginnings grew a worldwide ministry that has used literature to proclaim God's love and disciple generation after generation. Cook Communications Ministries is committed to personal discipleship—to helping people of all ages learn God's Word, embrace his salvation, walk in his ways, and minister in his name.

Opportunities—and Crisis

We live in a land of plenty—including plenty of Christian literature! But what about the rest of the world? Jesus commanded, "Go and make disciples of all nations" (Matt. 28:19) and we want to obey this commandment. But how does a publishing organization "go" into all the world?

There are five times as many Christians around the world as there are in North America. Christian workers in many of these countries have no more than a New Testament, or perhaps a single shared copy of the Bible, from which to learn and teach.

We are committed to sharing what God has given us with such Christians.

A vital part of Cook Communications Ministries is our international outreach, Cook Communications Ministries International (CCMI). Your purchase of this book, and of other books and Christian-growth products from Cook, enables CCMI to provide Bibles and Christian literature to people in more than 150 languages in 65 countries.

Cook Communications Ministries is a not-for-profit, self-supporting organization. Revenues from sales of our books, Bible curriculum, and other church and home products not only fund our U.S. ministry, but also fund our CCMI ministry around the world. One hundred percent of donations to CCMI go to our international literature programs.

. . . Around the World

CCMI reaches out internationally in three ways:

· Our premier International Christian Publishing Institute (ICPI) trains leaders from nationally led publishing houses around the world to develop evangelism and discipleship materials to transform lives in their countries.

· We provide literature for pastors, evangelists, and Christian workers in their national language. We provide study helps for pastors and lay leaders in many parts of the world, such as China, India, Cuba, Iran, and Vietnam.

· We reach people at risk—refugees, AIDS victims, street children, and famine victims—with God's Word. CCMI puts literature that shares the Good News into the hands of people at spiritual risk—people who might die before they hear the name of Jesus and are transformed by his love.

Word Power—God's Power

Faith Kidz, RiverOak, Honor, Life Journey, Victor, NexGen — every time you purchase a book produced by Cook Communications Ministries, you not only meet a vital personal need in your life or in the life of someone you love, but you're also a part of ministering to José in Colombia, Humberto in Chile, Gousa in India, or Lidiane in Brazil. You help make it possible for a pastor in China, a child in Peru, or a mother in West Africa to enjoy a life-changing book. And because you helped, children and adults around the world are learning God's Word and walking in his ways.

Thank you for your partnership in helping to disciple the world. May God bless you with the power of his Word in your life.

For more information about our international ministries, visit www.ccmi.org.